# Times P...

## Memories
### Of
## A BRISTOL BOY

## LEON PAICE

White Tree
Books

First published in 1996
by White Tree Books, Bristol

ISBN 1 900178 65 6

Typeset and printed by The Longdunn Press, Bristol.

# CHAPTER 1

"Leon, if you do not stop shrugging your shoulders the habit will grow on you." Those were the first words that I can remember my mother speaking to me. At three years of age what else would I do to move the braces back up on my shoulders? I was riding my "Mickey Mouse" bike at the time and needed my hands to steer the bike clear of the legs of the table and chairs. Most little boys in those days wore short trousers with a pair of braces to keep them up. Should the braces be slack, they would keep on slipping down over the shoulders. Usually, boys went into "long 'uns" (full-length trousers) at an age between twelve and fourteen years and dispensed with braces, to wear a waist belt with a letter "S" fastener to keep them up.

I must have taken heed of my mother's warning or the offending braces were regularly tightened up, as I did not grow up constantly shrugging my shoulders. This little bit of drama in my early childhood occurred in the front room of my Uncle Stan's house in Dale Street. This street ran parallel to Hill Street, and was the next one of many long streets and roads which made up the district of St. Paul's. Uncle Stan was one of my mother's four brothers; the other three were Cyril, Arthur, and Wilfred. I was staying at Uncle Stan's house because of some problem at near-by Hill Street. I learned in later years that it was because there was some illness within the Paice family and that I stayed with Uncle Stan for a number of weeks. My Paice family shared No. 8 Hill Street with the Sheen family. Aunt Rene was my mother's younger sister and with her husband Frank and their five children plus our family of seven persons, a total of fourteen persons lived at No. 8. Mother had another sister, Gladys, who was the eldest, my Aunt Gladys lived in Goodhind Street off Pennywell Road.

I was born up at the Royal Infirmary and after the customary six weeks had passed, I was baptised at St. Clement's Church, and named Leon Wilfred. The church used to stand at the junction of Newfoundland Street and Holton Street. I believe the church was badly damaged during the Bristol blitz and fell into disuse. Nothing now remains, the ground was taken up to build the start of the motorway. No. 8 Hill Street was one of a long line of Victorian houses, terraced and built on three floors. The Sheen family occupied part of the house, having a living room, two bedrooms and sharing the kitchen-cum-washing-room and backyard. My family had the same number of rooms plus a small box-room, which was situated above the kitchen. This room was used as a

Grandfather Richard Paice and grandmother, Ellen Jane at 49 Hill Street, St Pauls, 1935.

Father Charles Paice and mother, Doris at Willinton Road, Knowle, c.1948.

Leon, mother and Dion at Willinton Road, 1938.

Father with daughter, Joyce aged five months, 1920.

4

bedroom by my older brother Donald. Our living room was in the rear of the house and overlooked the backyard.

On the backyard wall hung a large tin bath. There was no bathroom and anyone wishing to take a bath would take this down and fill it with hot water from the washing boiler in the kitchen. The adults probably took their baths in a locked living-room. Us kids were bathed out in the backyard in the summer and indoors in the winter. There was one lavatory in the backyard.

I never cared very much to walk through the dark passage-way to or from the front door. That is, on my own. I did not like the poorly lit interior full of mysterious shadows, and the thought of some ghostly apparition appearing was always uppermost in my mind. So, once I had entered the front door it was my best foot forward to reach the safety of the living room. Likewise, if I wanted to go out to the street to play, it was a scramble to get clear of the passage-way as soon as possible. The house was gas-lit and the ground floor passage-way was not the only portent of doom and gloom. The stairs ascended through the middle of the house and were not lit at all. Going up to bed was always a dash, definitely no hanging about. The bedrooms spelt safety from whatever lurked in the eerie gloom of the stairs. As far as I can remember, the whole street was gas-lit, houses and the street lamps. Strangely though, in the next street, East Street, there was an electricity sub-station. The reason that electricity had not been installed in Hill Street and others was probably that the area was condemned and due for slum clearance. Towards the end of 1937, the clearance had started and families were on the move. Some went to new estates at Knowle and Southmead. The Paice and Sheen families were on the short list . . .

# CHAPTER 2

The Hill Street houses were consecutively numbered up one side, from the Newfoundland Street end, to the Ropewalk end at No. 28, then back down the other side and finished at No. 56, back at Newfoundland Street. My grandparents lived opposite at No. 49. At the Newfoundland Street end there were two large sheds with wide wooden doors, one shed each side on each corner. One shed was used as a holding shed for cows; the other was a slaughter-house where the animals were dispatched and the meat sold in the butcher's shop close by in Newfoundland Street. It was normal practice any day, except Sundays, to see the holding shed's doors fly open and a cow being dragged across the road by a rope round its neck to its slaughter. The poor animal would disappear behind the doors which were then shut with a loud bang. Sometimes the struggling animal managed to break free and ran up the street towards the Ropewalk, with the handlers in hot pursuit. The Ropewalk was a fenced-off stretch of concrete which ran from the Wade Street bridge across the top of Holton Street, Dale Street, Hill Street and East Street and finished opposite the Broad Weir Baths.

Under this stretch of concrete road ran the river Froom, known to the locals as the "Danny". It flowed under the Ropewalk, took a bend and emerged to the daylight, but only briefly, near the Tower Hill area, continuing its flow underground until it reached the Centre and then emerged once again to join the river at the Floating Harbour. My mother could remember when the Ropewalk area was open river banks before the river was covered over. During the long, hot summer evenings, the locals often sat along the river banks, with cooling jugs of ale or cider at their sides and sang songs to the music of banjos and piano-accordions. It was on the stretch of concrete, the Ropewalk, St. Matthias end, that we stored all manner of rubbish materials in readiness for bonfire-night. Usually, the kids started collecting weeks ahead, old chairs, wooden boxes, bundles of paper, cardboard boxes, anything to add to the ever growing pile. The big night arrived and the pile was made much higher by the last minute addition of old bits of carpet, furniture, the odd car tyre. To ensure a quick hold, the pile was doused with paraffin at the base, then a match thrown in to ignite the mass. Much excitement prevailed; and one big bonfire with fireworks was always the night of the year eagerly looked forward to by children and adults alike. But one year things got out of hand, for the pile of burning rubbish was so high that the flames were licking the branches of the trees which were close by on the Ropewalk. The fire brigade was called out to dampen the fire down. Naturally this added a bit more excitement for the kids.

When we were kids we never had many toys to play with, as we didn't have the money to buy them. So we made our own devices. With two old pram wheels and an axle, plus a large wood fruit box and two long pieces of wood for the shafts, and some nails, we made a cart. Carts were used for other purposes than play, such as trundling round the streets and shovelling up horse manure, of which there was always a fair amount in the streets of St. Paul's, as there were many horse-and-carts working the streets in those days. We sold the manure to budding gardeners at two pence per bucketful. Another money making scheme was to go round the houses collecting empty glass jam-jars. When we had collected a couple of dozen, we carted them home, washed them and loaded up the cart with the clean jars. Off we then pushed the cart round to Holton Street to the pickling factory, selling the jars at one penny for a two-pound jar and a halfpenny for a one-pound jar. The jars were used at the factory to hold various pickles such as onions, gerkins etc.

A toy often used by the kids was a metal "hoop", an old cycle wheel with the spokes removed and used with or without a tyre. The cycle wheel was hit with a short stick held in the hand and "hooped" along the road or wherever one was playing at the time.

Another great toy was a kind of trolley ride. A "Dandy" was made with a short plank of wood and four pram wheels plus a short length of rope and a four inch metal bolt to make a steering pivot, for the front wheels. Depending on what length of plank was used, two kids sat astride the "Dandy". The front chap steered by means of the short rope fixed to the pivot bar and pulled to the direction desired. The momentum was initiated by a third chap who pushed like mad and then jumped on to the back of the conveyance when the desired speed was reached. Two axles would be needed to make a "Dandy". The rear one "fixed" and the front one set to a free bar which allowed to turn on the four inch bolt. One afternoon my youngest brother, Dion and I were "hooping" along the Ropewalk and ran down on to the traffic road which ran parallel and were nearly hit by a passing car. Miraculously, the car screeched to a halt and we escaped injury. People rushed out from their houses to see what had happened. There was a shaking car driver, and two young boys scarpering off down the road. Dion and I did not intend to hang about, we were off along toward Holton Street to make our roundabout way home. Word had travelled from the Ropewalk by the householders down to Hill Street, and by the time the news had reached the Paice household it had changed out of all proportion. "Mrs. Paice, quick, your two youngsters have been knocked down by a car and are injured." Mother ran up to the scene of the accident and discovered no mangled bodies. Mother did see the car being driven away by the companion of the driver who had avoided an accident by quick thinking to apply his brakes in time. The poor chap was so shaken that he could not take the wheel to drive on. A very relieved mother made her way back down Hill Street. We expected a good hiding for nearly causing a nasty accident, not to mention the terrible state that we had inflicted on the unfortunate driver. But mother was so relieved that there were no injuries, we both received a good telling off and made to stay indoors for the rest of the day.

# CHAPTER 3

At this point it would be a good idea to give the names of all the Paice family. Father, Charles Richard born 18.2.1893. Mother, Doris Marjorie born 30.1.1900. Children . . . Joyce Doreen born 5.6.1921, Donald Arthur Richard born 1922, Keith John born 1925, Vernon Garth born 2.4.1927, Leon Wilfred born 3.5.1929, Dion Gerald born 25.5.1931. Sadly, Keith died of meningitis in 1929 when he was only 4 years of age and, as this was the year I was born, I never knew him. I have a photograph of Keith, taken with Joyce and Donald. It must have been taken shortly before Keith fell ill. I treasure this photograph very much. Keith was buried in a grave at Greenbank Cemetery. The grave belonged to my Uncle Stan. Also in the grave were Uncle Stan's first wife, Jesse and a little girl of theirs, who died at a young age. In those days meningitis was a dreaded disease, as it is now even though there are modern drugs to help fight it.

Opposite us in Hill Street lived my grandparents, Richard and Ellen Jane. Richard was born 14.7.1862 in Ryde, on the Isle of Wight. Ellen was born 19.12.1863 in Bristol. Their children were Annie, Herbert, Rose, Charles Richard, Florence, Violet, Alice and Louise. Annie left home to go to the South Coast to live and work, becoming a manageress in a Woolworths store in either Southampton or Portsmouth. I do not know whether she married or not. My father's youngest sister, Rose was my aunt before, and after, she had married my Uncle Stan. Aunt Rose and Uncle Stan were married in 1940. They had twin sons, Maurice and Bernard. Another son, Trevor, followed a few years later. Uncle Stan's children by his first wife were Jessie, Evelyn, Stanley, Clifford and Phillip.

In those days, Bristol had more than a fair share of cinemas. All told, counting venues in the outlaying suburbs, there were approximately 45 picture houses. A few of the music hall theatres, such as the Empire and the Hippodrome, showed movie pictures at times, but lacked the atmosphere of a proper cinema. The nearest cinema to Hill Street was in Newfoundland Street just round the corner. It was named The Magnet, and a fairly new venue with good modern comfortable seating, with reasonable low admission prices. There were cinemas in Old Market; there was also the Regent in Lower Castle Street, the News Theatre in or near Castle Ditch; with the Empire Theatre in Carey's Lane. There was the Metropole Cinema just a little further away, up towards the beginning of Ashley Road. As kids we loved going to the pictures or the

Joan's mother and father:
Edward George Wheadon and
Ivy Victoria, 1928.

The author's brothers
Keith and Donald with
sister Joyce, 1928.

"penny rush" as we called it. We were entertained by Tom Mix, Roy Rogers, Buck Jones, Gene Autry to name just a few of our "good-guys" or "our men". Strangely enough, I cannot remember any of the names of the "bad guys" or "their men" as we called them. I would not be surprised should anyone else of my age not remember them either. When a cowboy film was being shown there were a lot of cheers for "our men" and plenty of boos for "the baddies". The din created by the excited young audience was often deafening. Not very often, but it did happen occasionally, the kids were given a small bag of sweets as they queued up outside the Magnet for the Saturday morning show. At the Vestry, the only free things one was liable to receive were fleas. The Vestry was a "dump" compared to the Magnet and much of the seating was on long wooden forms. The fleas did not have to jump very far between the seated customers. But some very good serials, like *Flash Gordon* and *The Clutching Hand*, were shown at the Vestry. The films always ended at a most exciting point, the audience left wondering what happened next. Exciting to watch week by week but itchy at times and the wooden forms were hard to the bottom; not like the plush seats of the Magnet. I remember, one Saturday afternoon, going with Vernon and Dion to the Empire to see *Lives of the Bengal Lancers*. Gary Cooper and Victor McGlagen were starring. It was a smashing film and when we had seen our round, my two brothers prepared to leave and make their way home but I said I was staying to see the film round again. Vernon and Dion left without me. When I arrived home some two hours later I was well and truly told off and sent to bed without any supper. But I did not mind as I felt it was all worth it and I had been eating all the evening anyway. Before we had gone in to the theatre we had called into the bakery shop next door to the Empire Theatre. Bristol Bakeries sold off their stale cakes and buns for a penny a bag. There were other goodies which we were able to buy cheaply such as a large bag of 'bits', which were purchased from Woolworths for a penny. This store in Castle Street sold their mangled boiled sweets, trodden-on chocolates, and stuck-together toffees and various sweets to us kids quite often. Those were the days!

It was probably through eating too many of Woolworth's goodies, that I required some dental treatment. I was about five years old and my mother had made an appointment for me at the newly opened Tower Hill Clinic Dental Department. I had to have a number of teeth extracted and I was not looking forward to this encounter with the unknown. It was my first dental visit. Mother, holding my hand, took me in to the reception room and I said that I wanted to go home. I was re-assured by some motherly words. Or I think I was re-assured. I did not know what to expect, and I am sure my heart was fluttering. A nurse in a large white coat came and asked my name. "Right Leon," she said as she took hold of my trembling hand, pulled me away from my mother and ushered me in to a white room with a large strange chair set in the middle of the floor. There were two white-coated men with a nurse. When I entered the room, panic took me and I decided that I did not want to play; so I tried a runner for the door, but the nurse collared me and carried me back to the chair, where I was unceremoniously dumped. The nurse wrapped a rubber apron around me and wedged a square bit of rubber between my teeth. I started to struggle, so she placed her hands under the apron and clasped my hands. As I struggled, I saw a large white cylinder behind the table with a length of rubber tubing. At the other end of the tube was a circular rubber pad. I was now struggling like mad. Horror upon horrors, one of the men was holding the horrible evil-smelling pad just above my face and I watched in morbid fear as the foul thing descended to cover my mouth and nose. As I struggled I could hear the two men talking about the current events in Europe, particularly Germany. They had been reading a newspaper when I was taken in to the room. One man thought there would soon be war in Europe, which transpired in a year or so. When I came round from the sleeping-gas I was crying and had been dreaming of ghosts. Then the nurse asked what I had been dreaming about. Why I said it, I do not know, but my answer was "a cow". Of course, later, the war came. I still remember my first visit to a dentist sixty years ago, and what the two men were talking about. I did more or less get used to going to the dentist's over the years, but I am still not properly at ease. There is something about a dentist's chair.

# CHAPTER 4

Late 1938 . . .

My father was working in the malt and hop room of Rogers' (Simmonds) brewery in Old Market. Each worker was entitled to a free beer allowance, and this two pints was often supplemented by some men who would lower a bucket on a rope in to the vat to obtain some extra beer. Later years the brewery closed down, and some men went to work at George's brewery in Bath Lane near Victoria Street.

Donald was an errand-boy, delivering meat for a butcher's shop in Clifton. Donald made his delivery rounds on his bicycle and sometimes took meat to the Bristol Zoo. My mother and sister Joyce did leather stitching work at home for Shattock & Hunter, whose workshop was in Frogmore Street near the Hatchet Inn.

Vernon was attending the "open-air" school at the Novers in

Knowle. I was attending the church school at St. Matthias-on-the-Weir. I remember at one Harvest Festival service, I was given the honour of leading the church choir procession and I swung an incense burner on a chain as the procession made its way toward the flower-bedecked altar. I felt very proud as I led the procession through the aisles of the church. The congregation sang "We Plough The Fields And Scatter". I was not a member of that church choir then, but I became a choirboy at St. Paul's church in Portland Square later at the age of eight years.

Black Rocks? I do not know whether this was the correct name for the place, but it was a nice spot just beyond the Eastville area and we kids often went there to play. One hot summer's day Vernon, Dion and I decided to take a walk to the Black Rocks. We took a bottle of water and a rubber-ball. It was quite a long walk and eventually we arrived there to take a short rest. Then we started throwing the ball to one another. Where we stopped was on a river bank with a public footpath running alongside and there was a really fast flowing river. I threw the ball to Dion who missed the catch and the ball fell toward the river. A tree had fallen down and was jutting outward from the bank into the river. The ball had got snaggelled up in the branches. Vernon called out "I will get it" and he started to crawl along the tree-trunk toward the ball. Vernon leaned out and stretched forward to retrieve the ball but he over-balanced and slid off the trunk and into the water. Vernon clung desperately to the branches calling out for help. None of us could swim and there was the very real danger that Vernon would be swept away and drowned. But help was at hand. A man walking along the footpath towards us instantly sized up the situation, sprang into action, raced forward and waded in to the river and grabbed Vernon by the hair and dragged him out to safety. The man asked Vernon if he was okay. We all received a telling-off for being so stupid for playing ball so near to a river. The man turned away to continue his walk along the footpath. Vernon took the few clothes off that he was wearing and spread them on the river-bank to dry off in the hot sun. Some hours later we arrived home and mother asked where we had been for such a long time? "Just out playing," we replied. No mention of Vernon's lucky escape, and mother never learned of this near-tragedy. I often think back of the dangers we placed ourselves in during the course of play and the yearning for excitement.

Another of our favourite play places was Brandon Hill and the Cabot Tower. There was a high wall around the monument, from four points of the wall were mounted large cannons. The cannons had been captured at the siege of Sebastapol during the Crimean War. Each cannon over-looked the wall by approximately six feet barrels. We would climb up on to the cannon-breech and walk along the barrel to the muzzle-end overlooking the steep downward slopes of the hill. Luckily not one of us fell off the cannon. The Tower itself had an entrance at the base where there was a metal turnstile. To gain admission one would have to put a half-penny in the slot, which allowed one person through at a time. Because we had no money, or did not wish to pay, we used to squeeze through the parallel-bars to get inside without paying. The bars were only about ten inches apart but it was quite easy for us to squeeze through. Yes! we were that skinny. Once through the turnstile a spiral flight of stone steps led up to the parapet where one had a fine view of the city and the channel waters in the distance. Some days we combined a Tower visit with a trip to the Bristol Museum at the top of Park Street. There was no entry charge for the Museum in those days, and there were many splendid things on view there. We spent many a happy hour at the Museum but the art gallery never seemed to hold our interest very much.

The nearest seaside resort was "Wesson", as all "Brissle" kids called it, and very occasionally we were taken there on an outing. The Sunday-schools ran an outing annually but some kids who did not regularly attend Sunday-school always made sure that they were present for a couple of Sundays prior to the annual outing, so that they would be included on the trip. Usually, when the trip was finished and done with, these Sunday-school "hangers-on" stopped going to Sunday-school classes until the next year's outing.

# CHAPTER 5

When I was old enough I left St. Matthias school and started at St. Paul's school. The entrance to the school was in Wilson Street. In the middle of Wilson Street was the back entrance to the Magnet cinema where the queue for the 'penny rush' formed up. I could go one of two ways to school from Hill Street up through Paul Street then turn right, in to Wilson Street and then walk for five minutes to the school entrance. Alternatively, I could turn right at the bottom of Hill Street and walk along Newfoundland Road until I reached Gideon Arch and then walk through the arch and passage-way which ended opposite the school entrance.

More often than not, I went the Gideon Arch way. Let me explain . . . At the entrance to the Arch was a sweet shop and outside stood a chewing gum machine. When a penny was inserted and the drawer pulled, two packets of 'Beechnut' chewing gum were delivered. There was a bonus. For every fourth penny inserted, the operator of the

13

machine could give the drawer another pull and two free packets of gum would be delivered. All passing kids always gave the chewing gum machine drawer a tug, just in case the last user had neglected to try another pull. It was remarkable how many purchasers never bothered, leaving the chance for a lucky pull to some passing kid, as once happened to me. But I was more than lucky one day. On my way to school, I gave the machine my customary tug and out came the drawer with two packets of gum. I was delighted at my luck. I returned the drawer and thought to give it another pull. Who knows, it may deliver again. The mechanism must have gone wonky, for it gave out again and again, and I finished up with ten free packets of 'Beechnut' chewing gum. I did think about going in to the shop to report the machine's crazy antics but did not bother as I would have been accused of messing about with the machine.

As I was now attending St. Paul's school I had a yearning to join the church choir so I went to see the choirmaster, Mr. Watson, who had me go up and down the scales. Two other boys from Hill Street, Royston Trotman and Charlie Ainsson, also came with me for the interview. All three of us were accepted and fitted out with cassock and surplice and shown our places in the choir stalls. I was a bit on the short side so my place was in the front row stall. Royston and Charlie were set in the middle stall. There was a financial side to consider too. The choir boys' pay was three pence per week, with additional payments for weddings and funerals. The choirmaster would pay us two pence per event, but a wedding was, sometimes, lucrative with a present from the bride and groom and perhaps a tanner (sixpence) as well. I never could remember the name of the vicar of St. Pauls, but I well remember the name of the vicar at St. Matthias. Dicky Bannister was a well regarded man in the community. Everyone liked him, I do not know whether his name was Richard or not. I believe the term "Dicky" was added to some vicars' names. Dicky Bannister was a good, caring man and always ready to help his parishioners, visiting and giving good advice. He often visited his young flock, who were in Ham Green Hospital with scarlet fever or some other contagious disease. During my stay at the hospital there were half a dozen kids there who lived in Hill Street or Dale Street. Dicky Bannister always brought comics and sweets. Patients taken to Ham Green Hospital would be stripped of all their clothes, and then immersed fully into a bath of disinfectant. This was normal practice as Ham Green was a hospital for infectious diseases. When patients were fit and well, clear of all infection, ready to go home, the disinfectant bath was repeated. Just to make sure, I suppose.

There was one little thing which Dicky Bannister did during his sermons which was a source of embarrassment to a few offenders, but

14

amused most of the congregation. It was when the odd person nodded off. Dicky Bannister would snap his fingers and point to the offender, whereupon the person would rejoin the congregation, alert again, but perhaps with a red face.

Back to St. Paul's school.

This was a Victorian structure and falling apart everywhere, the playground was simply a piece of stony, rough ground. A high wall in the middle of the playground segregated boys from girls. It was the practice of the boys, in winter, to lob snowballs over the wall at the girls. This continued until one day a snowball containing a sharp stone cut a girl's head. From that day all snowballing was banned on school premises as there were too many stones in the playgrounds. The penalty for transgressors was four of the best. The odd snowball was still being thrown over the wall, though. The parish of St. Paul's was densely populated, as was St. James'. It was in 1830 that St. Paul was consecrated to take in the ever-swelling population of St. James' parish. St. Paul's church is now redundant as is Holy Trinity in West Street. St. Clement's, another small church, was badly damaged during an air-raid. St. Paul's had some fire damage during the blitz and the church registers of births, marriages and deaths, were destroyed. St. Clement's church is where my parents were married, in 1920. I was baptised there 5.6.1929. Rose Paice was my godparent.

# CHAPTER 6

Although my grandfather, Richard Paice lived just opposite us in Hill Street I can remember seeing him only once. The occasion was a street party to celebrate the golden jubilee of King George and Queen Mary in 1936. Down the centre of the street was a line of tables and the kids sat down to a feast of cakes, jelly and fizzy drinks. Ice cream was available. The kids wore fancy paper hats as did a number of adults. The street was straddled and bedecked with colourful bunting and flags. I sat at the table which was opposite my grandparents' house, and that was the first and only time I ever saw my grandfather, for he was stood in his doorway with Granny Paice watching the proceedings. I did not see much of my Granny Paice: I think, no more than half a dozen times. Grandfather Richard was fairly tall, a six footer, but Granny Paice was little. One could say, little by name, and little by nature, for Granny's maiden name was Little.

It was in the times that my mother and my sister Joyce stitched leather work at home for Shattock and Hunter. They sat at the living room table

15

with their feet in the stirrups of a pair of clams. These clams jaws held the pieces of leather together whilst they were stitched together; buckles and other various bits of leather were added as the work progressed. The work was mainly for horse harnesses, but my mother often stitched saddle girths, and other heavy harness, which was called black harness, which was really a man's work, for it was heavy and hard. Mother's father, Arthur Edward William Wall, was born in Kingswinford, Staffordshire. He was a journeyman saddler, who finally settled down to live in Bristol. My mother was born in Sevior Street, Stapleton. 30.1.1900.

When my mother was 14 years of age, she went into the leather stitching trade. It was probably in her blood, for the skill was quickly learnt and mother could tackle any type of leather stitching, including saddles. To watch my mother stitch was enthralling, her fingers flew as the awl pierced the leather and two needles pulled the waxed thread through the leather. Buckles were added as the work progressed. Mother must have stitched hundreds of Sam Browne belts for Army officers. Even I, wearing a small apron, played my small part in the operations. I made the threads for the stitchers. This is how they were made. There was a brass hook screwed into the wall and a marker on the floor. I would stand on the marker and take a turn of hemp round the hook, back walk to the marker, repeating this move three times so that I had six lengths of hemp. Each length was waxed as it was looped around the hook. The hemp was cut at this stage. I then waxed and rolled the whole strands together, rolling into one thick five foot long waxed thread. The thread was rolled against the leather apron which I was wearing.

The stitcher used two needles to each thread, a needle to each end. The awl would be held in the right hand, a needle held in the right hand fingers and the other needle held in the left hand fingers. The leather would be pierced with the awl, and the needles pushed through the hole at opposite sides of the leather. The thread would then be pulled to equal lengths nice and taut to form the stitch in the leather. This action was repeated until the piece of work was completely stitched, the thread was knotted and then cut. At some time, during the war, my mother and sister Joyce worked for Lennards boot and shoe makers in Milk Street. One item they stitched were white high leather boots for Russian soldiers in the snows of the Russian war-front.

Christmases came and Christmases went. When we were young kids we never had a lot of presents, just a few small toys, such as a tin clockwork motor-car, a mouth-organ or a modestly priced clock-work train set. On a good year we could receive as an extra, a sixpenny Fry's chocolate "selection-box". This was a large flat cardboard box which contained two different bars of chocolate, a packet of jelly sweets, a

16

liquorice pipe, a packet of candy cigarettes, and some rolled-up liquorice laces. The box would contain a few paper puzzles; the box itself, when empty, revealed a printed-on game and could be Ludo, Snakes and Ladders or even Draughts. We also had a bag of nuts and a couple of apples and oranges.

The church choir would go out carol-singing to collect money for the church funds. We always headed to the area where the residents were reckoned to be well off, like the large houses in Stokes Croft or up along the Gloucester Road. Mr Watson was in charge and after we sang a number of carols he received money from the householders. At some houses, we were invited in for a warm by the fireside. The boys were given hot cups of cocoa and hot mince pies, while Mr Watson partook of a glass of sherry, or even whisky, and was given as much as five shillings at some houses for the church. After a round of the district we made our way back to the church, all well pleased with our collection. We were all merry and happy. By the time we arrived back at the church it could be said that our choir-master was the merriest of the lot of us, for he had drunk several "warming-up drinks".

One Spring morning I awoke to the discomfort of a very sore throat and as the day progressed, I steadily felt worse and my temperature increased considerably. I really felt ill. In the evening when my father came home from work he took one look at me and said, "you look terrible, you are boiling-up, I had better take you up to the out-patient department of the Infirmary." The Infirmary was about ten minutes' walk from Hill Street, and my father probably got up there in less time than that. I was carried well wrapped-up in a blanket and we took a seat in the out-patients room to await a doctor. After a short wait a doctor came to have a look at me. He said, "you look all hot and bothered young man, let's see what is troubling you." He asked me to open my mouth as wide as I could and looked down my throat. "H'm," he exclaimed, "a very nasty throat you've got," and he took some swabs of my throat. He then went away to have the swabs tested. He returned some thirty minutes later and told my father the result of the test.

The doctor said one word, "DIP", which settled it straight away. I had the dreaded Diptheria. I would have to be taken down to the Isolation Hospital at Ham Green as soon as possible. Before my father left me he gave me a "tanner" (sixpence) to cheer me up. The nurse went with me in the ambulance down to Ham Green at Pill, some miles outside Bristol. The nurse wrapped my "tanner" in cotton-wool for safe keeping and put it in my pocket. When I arrived at the hospital I was given a disinfectant bath and put to bed. My belongings were put in a bedside locker, including my plug of cotton-wool with my precious "tanner". After two weeks I had recovered and was due to go home. I

17

was dipped in the disinfectant bath again and then dressed in my clothes, which had been also cleaned and disinfected. I cleared out my locker, looking for my ball of cotton-wool and my "tanner" but it was missing. Probably what happened was that the ball of cotton-wool was thrown out by a cleaner, who thought it was a ball of waste. But I was not worried too much, after all I was on my way home. My mother and Aunt Gladys came down to fetch me home from the hospital. We travelled by train from Pill to Parson Street station, then boarded a tram-car to take us to Old Market: a short walk down Carey's Lane through to Broad Weir and we were home.

# CHAPTER 7

Back to school . . .

My teacher was running a competition in aid of charity. He had counted a very large number of dried peas and placed them in a glass jar, which he kept on show on his desk. The jar had been sealed. The competition was for pupils to guess the number of peas, each guess to cost a half-penny each. There was no limit to the number of guesses made as long as each guess was paid for. The winner would be the pupil who had correctly guessed the number of peas or the nearest number. There were three prizes, first prize two-and-sixpence, one shilling for the next nearest guess, and sixpence for the next nearest again. The competition had been going for a few weeks, each pupil's name and their estimated number of peas was recorded in a exercise book by the teacher. Excitement was growing daily. Who was to be the lucky winner? I had not had a guess so far and was beginning to wonder if I should invest a couple of half-pennys. There seemed to be, and probably were, hundreds of peas in the jar. Anyway. One morning our teacher logged the names and numbers in his book and to give some interest to the project mentioned the name of the pupil with the closest number guessed so far. Of course, no mention was made of the actual number itself. Yours truly got to thinking. Was it not time for me to have a couple of guesses? The teacher had stirred up my interest by quoting the nearest pupil so far. George was the boy's name and I simply asked him how many guesses he had made and his estimated numbers. He had made only one guess and estimated seven hundred and sixty two peas, or something in that order. I cannot remember the exact number now, as it was so many years ago. What I did was to guess two numbers, one number ten up, and the other number ten below George's estimate. I thought I had a good chance of winning the prize, or even a consolation.

As it turned out I won the two-and-sixpence, as one of my numbers was even closer than poor George's. It could be said that my "calculated" risk payed off. Even in my youth I liked to think that I used my head in most matters.

The residents of St. Paul's were good neighbours to one another even though they were thought a rough lot. There were rows and squabbles at times between neighbours, nearly always over children, but once they were done with, all was soon forgotten. Nobody seemed to hold grudges for ever, as the case is now, on the council estates and where vandalism, burglary, and attacks on persons are all too frequent.

The Sally Army used to march up Hill Street, stop and form a circle where the band played hymns and the residents joined in with the singing. I remember well when I lived in Hill Street, on Sundays, when the air was filled with the peals of church bells from all over the city. I always thought of the bells in those days as an inspiring, if somewhat awesome, noise.

When my grandfather Wall died, he was laid out in his coffin in our living room. On the morning of the funeral, all the kids – Paices and Sheens – were taken in to the living room where grandfather Wall lay and we were all made to kiss him as a last goodbye. It was a frightening thing to have to do and when the afternoon came and the hearse drew up outside the house, all of us kids were locked up in the Sheen's room and prevented from seeing the coffin being carried out of the house. I could never see the reason behind this. We could see and kiss him in his coffin but not be allowed to watch as he was carried out of the house? Very strange. The internment took place at Fishponds. My granny Wall had died some years previously. I cannot remember ever seeing her.

I think of the past, when my grandfather Wall worked at Shattock and Hunter in Frogmore Street and he walked home to Fishponds via the Horsefair, Milk Street, Newfoundland Street and so up to Fishponds. We sometimes went to meet him in Milk Street on Friday evenings. He would give us each a half-penny, which we spent in the local sweet shop.

# CHAPTER 8

1938. Summer, and the occupiers of No. 8 Hill Street received notice that they had been allocated houses on the new housing estates. The Sheen family were destined for Southmead and the Paice family were soon to be off to Knowle. The new house for us was a parlour type at No. 110, Willinton Road, Filwood Park. Both families had a week's notice to quit and take up their new tenancies. The big day came and the Paices were going first, so the Sheens were able to give us a hand in loading up the removal-van. To save on bus-fares, Father, Vernon, Dion and myself travelled up to Knowle in the van. Mother and Joyce went up by bus and Donald rode his cycle. The nearest bus-stop to Willinton Road was the last stop in Melvin Square, and it took a ten minute walk to get to Willinton Road. Donald took about three quarters of an hour to reach our new home. We arrived at Willinton to see a brick-built house with a front and rear garden, the rear one being quite large. The van was unloaded, most stuff being left in the front garden or on the pavement to be moved in later. It took a while to get sorted out. There were three bedrooms, bathroom, an airing-cupboard upstairs, while downstairs were the front parlour, living-room with a Welsh-dresser and another airing-cupboard, and there was the kitchen with a larder. The stairs were immediately behind the front door in the hall-way. There was an iron gas stove and a metal boiling washer-tub out in the kitchen. The kitchen floor was of bare stone concrete and the other rooms had wood floors. The one and only lavatory was in the bathroom upstairs. There was a gas water heater (Geyser) over the bath. This Geyser always ignited with a tremendous bang and was a bit worrying at times. But we much preferred this method of taking a bath to the old tin bath procedure of Hill Street. The largest bedroom was for the four boys, smallest bedroom for Joyce, and a medium size bedroom for our parents. When all was sorted and things generally settled down we started to relax and take a rest. Mother sat down on the stairs and started to cry. It was all too much for her moving away from her friends and neighbours. We all gathered around her and with some cheery chatter and funny remarks, mother soon bucked up and was her old self again. It was not expected for our mother to stay down in the dumps anyway, as she was pretty tough and could usually face any adversity.

Father now had to catch a bus to his work in the brewery down town. His starting time was seven o'clock in the morning so he had to do a ten minute walk to Melvin Square each morning, then catch a bus to Old Market and so to Simmonds brewery. To be on time he left home each morning at six fifteen. Father finished work at five thirty each evening, Monday to Friday, and he usually arrived home at six thirty. On Saturdays he worked until one o'clock.

Even though my father worked in a brewery he would still like to ride Vernon's bike down to the Happy Landings pub each evening for a pint. If mother fancied a drink, he would bring one home for her. Donald rode his bike up to Clifton for his work in the butcher's shop. He left home pretty early too. Even though he had the bike, it was a long ride up to Clifton, and must have taken the best part of a hour. Donald did deliveries for the butchers and sometimes delivered meat to Bristol Zoo for the animals.

Off and on, mother and Joyce did work for Shattock and Hunter. My sister married Joe Lawrence, who was a charge hand at the leather works in Frogmore Street. He was the 'cutter outer' of the work to be stitched and brought the work home to Willinton Road for mother and Joyce to stitch. As the Novers school was just some ten minutes or so walking distance from our home, Vernon was able to walk to school now.

Dion and I attended Ilminster Avenue school in the juniors, ten minutes or so walk from Willinton Road.

Joyce complained one morning of stomach pains which grew worse as the day went on. It was late in the evening that a doctor was called to have a look at her. Appendicitis was diagnosed, my sister was rushed off to hospital for an operation. The appendix removed, Joyce made a good recovery and was soon back home with us.


# CHAPTER 9


September, 1939. The War had come, rationing started, men were being called up to serve in the forces. Strips of brown sticky paper were stuck across the glass in windows, and everyone was issued with a gas-mask. The masks had to be taken everywhere. At school, everyone had to practice putting on their gas-mask. I hated the rubbery smell. It reminded me of my first dentist's visit.

Donald went into the Army as a gunner in the Royal Horse Artillery, and later went overseas to India and Burma. Joe, my brother-in-law, went into the Army, too, and served as a gunner on board merchant ships. He was on a merchant ship in a large convoy to Russia during the War. The convoy consisted of fifty merchant ships with a flotilla of destroyers to guard them from enemy ships and submarines. They were carrying vital supplies to the Russians and it was a desperate voyage, the middle of a very severe winter and the ships had to sail through U-boat-infested seas. Many were sunk or badly damaged with a great loss of lives. The remainder got through to their destination. Fifteen ships did not make it. Joe survived the trip, and when he came home on leave he would tell us of the hazardous voyages. He told us of one voyage to America, when an American destroyer fired on what they thought to be an enemy plane; unfortunately, it was one of theirs, which came down in the sea nearby.

Mother and Joyce were now travelling to town to do work at Shattock and Hunters on the Centre, at Frogmore Street, as there was nobody to bring the work up to them at Knowle.

Before I went to school each morning, I did the housework for mother and did any required shopping on the evenings after school. Dion and I were settled in to our new school at Ilminster Juniors, which was a modern brick built-school for the ever growing population of Knowle West. It was a large well spaced-out building set in a quadrangle of green lawn. The class-room doors opened to flat smooth concrete play-grounds. There was a long wide path from the school entrance up to the class-rooms.

I became the milk-monitor and each morning at about nine-thirty I went to each class-room and noted down the number of bottles of milk required. I then walked down to the school gates to meet the milkman on his float and clambered aboard. He drove around the perimeter of the school grounds, calling at each classroom door to off-load the number of bottles required. We collected empties as we made our way around. Afterwards, I went back to my classroom to continue my lessons.

The school air-raid shelter was built below the grass surround of the playground at a depth of ten feet. The city air-raid sirens were tested now and again. The school pupils were quickly, but orderly, marched to the shelter by the teachers. One morning the air-raid siren was sounding and we all marched off to the shelter. No sooner had we all been installed in the shelter then there was the drone of a solitary enemy aircraft high above the city. Then the explosion of a bomb was heard. It wasn't too long for the all-clear siren to sound. It had been just one plane, which made off after it dropped the single bomb. We marched back to our classrooms, the general chatter being "I wonder where the bomb landed?" Later it was learned that the bomb had fallen in a road at the bottom of Careys Lane. The explosion set two buses on fire and caused considerable damage to nearby houses. Some people were killed. One lady killed was Mrs Bird, whom I knew from the days when we lived in Hill Street. It was said at the time that the plane's target was the "Whitehouse" which was on the Centre. It was also said, rumour or not, that the "Whitehouse" was an alternative war headquarters for Winston Churchill, should his London H.Q. be bombed. It was also well known that the "Whitehouse" had many well built chambers deep below ground level. As it was, the lone plane sneaked up the Bristol Channel and caught the city unawares. It practically dropped its bomb the same time as the warning siren was sounding, and the bomb landed half a mile away from the Centre.

At Ilminster Juniors, we were taught the basic three "Rs". We went on to more interesting subjects at Connaught Senior school, where I transferred at the age of eleven years and was soon in to carpentry, gardening, cricket, football, and physical education. The headmaster's name was Russet. He was a tough man. He needed to be – there were quite a number of rough diamonds at the school – and the job would not have suited a weak man.

Knowle West was a tough area, tough parents with tough kids.

Three other teachers were "Sammy" Smart, Mr. Barnard and Bert Blake, who was our sports teacher. I believe Bert once played football for Bristol Rovers.

"Tawkin Brissle" – Bristol folk's own dialect – was very amusing to outsiders. As you read the next paragraph, I will lapse into a bit of "Brissle Tawk", ay. Near where we lived in Willinton Road, was the Whitchurch airfield. There were two farms near the air-field. One belonged to a farmer named Hazell, who owned some apple-orchards as well. The boys in our gang were prone to a bit of scrumping from farmer Hazell's apple-orchards. One morning we were caught in the act and kids were running in all directions. Some of us ran up Airport Road. As we reached the junction with Creswicke Road, another group of kids were on their way down to the farms, and when they saw us in flight they called out "whir az de bin den?" We replied, "weave bin pinchin du appels offal' ol' 'Aysells treeze." "Didee cash ay den?" they asked. "Yeh, e nurlay cawt us," we yelled back. "Sew ede beher not gover relse e ul ave ay." We called out, "yer, wahz fink den?" "We cawt a gert big nute in du duckpon' behine du airfiel' wheeze gonah cawl im Desprit Dan." I used to think that our speech was unique, until I was older, and travelled about in various other counties, and listened to the local dialects.

A stream flowed alongside Airport Road. We fished out sticklebacks and tadpoles; with the newts from the duckpond, we took them home in a jam-jar to keep in an old tin bath out in our back garden. The average age of kids in our gang was thirteen years, and we had not yet heard in those days about being environmentally friendly and look after the wildlife. We all know better now. That's how it should be, and I wish us kids, and adults, in those days had heard of the word conservation.

The War was in its second year and occasionally we saw the fighter planes which were stationed at the airfield. The pilots were Polish. It was not possible to see the planes on the ground for they were too well camouflaged but when they took off it was a lovely sight to see them. One day we were walking around the airfield perimeter. When we came to the duckpond we saw the tail-end of a fighter plane sticking out of the water. The plane was probably damaged and as it came down to land, had nosed down in to the duckpond. The duckpond was on the other side of Whitchurch Lane and was in the flight path of the airport. There were many flights of Dakotas, in and out of the airport, and they sometimes came in very low over the houses in Willinton Road so low at times, it was a wonder the planes' wheels missed the chimney pots. The natural slope of the ground was downward and there was one more road between Willinton and the Airport Road and that was Alard Road. In the surroundings fields, and right over to Washing Pound Lane, were batteries of anti-aircraft guns. The biggest guns were considered to be at Washing Pound Lane. There was a search-light unit at this location also. During the night-time air-raids the guns fired at the enemy planes caught in the criss-crossed beams of the searchlights. We always knew when the guns at Washing Pound Lane were firing because of the resounding crack they made. The battery Commander must have shouted through a megaphone during the general din, as we often heard his command "Fire".

Our family shared a shelter up in the Cashman's garden. The shelter was called an Anderson shelter, which was made of corrugated metal and half buried under the garden soil. One night, it seemed that the raid was being directed at Knowle, and most probably at the airport, for it was a very intense raid with many bombs and incendiaries falling over the airport area and the houses and other buildings in Knowle. The anti-aircraft guns were blazing away, and much shrapnel was falling earthwards. Many places were set on fire by the incendiary bombs. Luckily, the ones that fell on the Cashman and Paice houses landed on the garden paths and were extinguished by turning a bucket of sand over on top of them. It was better to use the sand method as water usually increased the intensity of the fire. The raid lasted some hours. The din and clatter was deafening, and if anyone said they were not scared, they would have been telling lies. There was always a whistling noise as a bomb came down and by this noise it could be calculated whether it was a distant impact or a near miss. Of course there was the explosion as well.

Those of us who were in the shelter had our lives given us, that night. There were Mrs Cashman, Tony, Mark, and my mother, Joyce, Vernon, Dion and myself in the shelter. There was a shrill whistle of a falling bomb and it sounded too close for comfort. We all cowered down on the floor of the shelter and waited, briefly, for the explosion to come. And come it did. There was a terrific explosion followed by a swishing noise and then a loud thud which shook the very ground around us. The next morning, when we emerged from the shelter, we saw a large chunk of concrete lying half embedded in the garden, and just five feet away from the shelter.

The bomb had fallen on Throgmorton Road, exploded and blew a piece of the road through the air to land in Cashman's garden. On its flight through the air, the piece of road, which could have weighed a couple of tons, clipped the corner off the Barry's house in Throgmorton

24

Road, leaving a gaping hole. The next morning Dion and I went souvenir hunting, for there were plenty of bits of shrapnel lying around in the roads. We took a look at the bomb crater in Throgmorton Road. The crater spread right across the road, from one pavement to the other. If that chunk of concrete had landed on the shelter we would all certainly have been killed. God took care of us that night. Many houses suffered fire damage and there were many unexploded incendiary bombs all over the place. There were a number of unexploded bombs for the bomb disposal squads to make safe. Many of these were buried in the soft soil of the airport's ground, failing to go off on impact. The massive chunk of concrete was still visible in Cashman's garden, when I moved away from Willinton Road in 1956.

## CHAPTER 10

The war continued . . . High up in the sky, circling the city, were hundreds of barrage balloons. They were normally used during daylight hours to deter low flying enemy aircraft from bombing the city. I cannot ever remember a plane hitting the balloon's wire hawser which was used to control the rise and lowering of the balloons. One night, at dusk, when the balloons were lowered, a violent thunderstorm developed over the city and before the balloons could be pulled down, lightning was striking one after the other. We watched from our upstairs windows the awesome sight as flaming balloons floated down to earth. Out of a total of perhaps a hundred balloons, twenty or so came down in flames. The balloons were anchored in open spaces all around the city. At Knowle there was a balloon in Melvin Square, and another up on the green at the top of Salcombe Road. I am not sure, but I think there was another balloon at the Novers. Vernon was working for a small outfit doing roofing and general painting and decorating work, and there was just three of them, two old men and Vernon plus of course the boss, by the name of Pledger. The yard was located at the Wells Road end of Redcatch Road. I was in my last days at school and spent much of the days in the school garden.

Mother and Joyce were still doing work for Shattocks, stitching Sam Browne belts and other various bits of leather work. Donald was in India, Joe still at sea, Father still helping to make beer, down at Simmonds brewery.

Dion was in his first year at Connaught Road school. As I have already written, I did the housework for my working mother before I went off to school. One morning I arrived late for school and, as was the custom, late arrivers had to report to the headmaster. I expected a good telling-off from Mr Russet but instead he gave me a penny to catch a bus at Melvin Square so that I could join my class who had already departed for the baths at Jubilee Road. I was hardly ever late for school and the headmaster knew that I was helping my mother by doing household chores. It was still wartime and allowances were made in deserving cases. The third day of May, 1943 was my fourteenth birthday and my last day at school. I was about to start work in earnest.

Vernon got me a job at Pledgers. I was to receive sixpence an hour for a forty hour week, less fourpence stamp money. This meant my take-home pay would be nineteen shillings and eightpence. I gave Mother seventeen shillings and I had two shillings and eightpence for myself. Not much, you might think, but a little money went a long way.

The cinema, fourpence; bar of chocolate two pence; boiled sweets two pence a quarter; for smokers, a packet of Woodbines for fivepence.

I did not use the bus for getting to work, I walked.

In those days, holidays were never taken by anyone in our household. So there was no saving money for that.

When I started work I was a short, skinny chap standing about four feet four inches high and weighed probably six stone. I really earned my pay at Pledgers as a general dogsbody, fetching and carrying for the older men. As the dogsbody I was sent with the hand cart all on my own to fetch materials as far away as Stokes Croft, and other places in Redcliff, even over the river to the Princes Street area. I fetched buckets of mortar, large sheets of glass, tins of paint. The cart was no small light vehicle either. It was a really heavy cumbersome large cart, it had three feet diameter wheels and shafts which a horse would have fitted in to.

I often felt like a small horse struggling to pull and push that cart. For instance, if there was a job to do down at the Rex Cinema in Bedminster, the cart would be laden with buckets of this, tins of that, tools, tarpaulins, and to complete the load, long extension ladders would be added. The men would not offer to help get the cart to the job, they went on ahead, by bus. Vernon had to ride his bike down to the site as he would need the bike to get home. I would get down to St. John's Lane by way of Redcatch Road, then down over Redcatch Hill, slanting the cartwheels in to the curb as I descended, then along St. John's Lane in to Bedminster, and along to the Rex Cinema. I thought the downward journey was crippling enough, but when the job was finished, the process was reversed, the cart loaded and I was on my own again, this time to push the cart all the way back and up the very steep Redcatch Hill, to get back to the yard. How I ever managed, I do not know but I did and perhaps that extremely hard slogging, is why I now suffer from rheumatics. If it meant getting back to the yard too late to do any work, Bert and George – would go straight home on the bus. Alternatively, if there was plenty of time left, then they would make their way back to the yard, by bus of course. I stayed in that job for nine months. I should have chucked it in much, much earlier.

# CHAPTER 11

The bombing of Bristol had eased off by the time I ceased work with Pledgers.

There was one particular air-raid which still sticks in my mind, and that was the one that took place on the night of Good Friday, – It was a concentrated attack on the centre of the city and intended to demoralize the inhabitants, as well as cause as much damage as possible, to the city's buildings. The first intention certainly did not work, but the second did. Many buildings were blown apart and reduced to rubble and also much damage was caused by buildings set ablaze by the incendiary bombs. Stores, shops, homes, churches, all were buildings that did not escape the downpour of bombs.

This raid sticks in my mind because on that night, Mother, Dion and I were visiting my mother's sister, our Aunt Gladys who lived in Pennywell Road, opposite the Claremont pub. We had been at the house all afternoon and evening and at about nine-thirty we decided to make tracks home, so we all said our good-nights to one another and off we went. The Lebeck Pub was where we headed for, which was in Stapleton Road, as the bus stop was near the pub. We heard the warning siren as we left Pennywell Road but decided to continue to the bus stop. As we were walking along Stapleton Road toward the Lebeck pub, flares were dropping from the sky. One further up the road had landed and was turning the night into daylight. Another flare had landed smack in the middle of Stapleton Road, and turning that area into light. Looking up West Street and beyond, towards town, there were many flares illuminating the sky, bombs were dropping and exploding all over the place. All hell was breaking loose. It was a very frightening situation to be in and we decided to run back to our Aunt Glady's house for shelter. "Quick, run on ahead and get to your Aunt's house and I'll follow on behind," said mother. "No fear," we replied, "we are waiting for you, we all go together." We half ran, walked, and stumbled as fast as we could back to Aunt Gladys's house. We arrived out of breath, shaking with fear, and joined our aunt's family who were sheltering below their stairs, as they had no garden, so no Anderson shelter. It seemed like an eternity before the morning dawned. The all-clear had sounded some hours beforehand but we waited until morning to go home.

After a bite of breakfast, we said our goodbyes again and set out for the bus in Stapleton Road, but this time the stop opposite Armoury Square. Looking toward town we saw a massive pall of smoke. Fires were still burning. No bus came, so we assumed that they were not running, perhaps they had been re-routed due to road damage. After waiting a while, we set off to walk home, or at least, part of the way. We walked up through West Street to Old Market and then toward Castle Street. It was terrible to see the damage. Castle Street was no more, flattened to the ground. Churches were burnt out. All around there was fire and destruction. Some fires were still burning or smouldering, and the roads were laced with fire-hoses. When we neared Castle Street, we saw that it was barricaded off, and we were told by an A.R.P. man that no one could pass due to the danger of falling masonry. So we by-passed that street and went down Tower Lane, turned right to go over St. Phillips bridge and reached there to find that the bridge had a whacking great hole in the middle, so we could not use that route either. The next and only way now to get to Victoria Street was to backtrack to the new road and Temple Way bridge over the water and then in to Victoria Street. So we turned round and walked back through the road where the church of St. Philips with St. Jacobs stands, and walked through to Temple Meads incline. There were no buses to be seen but we were lucky to get a taxi which took us home to Knowle. The rest of the family were worried sick and were relieved to see us home, all in one piece. We told them of the terrible damage downtown. The family had not been to bed or taken shelter, as the raid was taking place more away in town. They had realized, though, that the town was copping it.

# CHAPTER 12

1944 . . . German prisoners-of-war were putting up prefabs along the main roads near the airport. That was from the Knowle airport entrance and right along the road to Wells Road. The prisoners laid concrete pavements all along the stretch of prefabs in that road. Some prisoners scratched their names and numbers in to the wet cement, a permanent record of their having been there. The pavements have been probably relaid over the years. All the prefabs were gradually pulled down and replaced with new houses along Airport Road. There are prefabs still standing in the St. George area however, and maybe other places as well in Bristol. In the road where I live at present, there used to be prefabs, now there are houses and bungalows. I live in a bungalow in this Inns Court area. When I moved away from the airport area in 1956, the names of the German prisoners who built the prefabs along the Airport Road could still be seen in the pavements.

It was also in 1944 that I left Pledgers to go and work in the sugar factory called the Brewers Invert, in Little Bishop Street, St. Pauls. My Uncle Stan was the foreman there. It was a heavy and hard job. Always, a sticky mess of a job and consistent. It was for the men, anyway. I was but a young lad, only fifteen years of age. My job was to make tea and keep the messroom clean and tidy, and run errands for fish and chips, cakes, cigarettes and other items for the men. Also I was the unofficial bookie's runner for the factory workforce. The bookie operated from his hairdressing shop in Grosvenor Road. I collected the bets each day as I made my rounds of the factory floors. On my rounds of the shops I took the bets in to the hairdressing shop and passed them over to the bookie's wife, who sometimes gave me a bob or a packet of cigarettes. The bookie used to give me a few quid on a Christmas time. When the chaps at the factory had a win, they always gave me something, depending on the size of the win.

Although the shop owner was a hairdresser by trade, he very rarely cut anyone's hair. He used to run his book from his living quarters above the shop and was rarely seen downstairs in the shop. He had an assistant, who worked the hairdressing side of things. The bookie's wife managed the shop counter, selling sundry goods such as combs, hair clips, and nets, hair creams, tobacco, cigarettes and etc. The bookie's operation was illegal. One day I walked in with the usual bundle of betting slips clasped in my hand but I knew straight away that there was something amiss, as there were two strangers behind the counter with the bookie's wife. I quickly stuffed the slips of paper into my overall pocket and calmly asked for a packet of cigarettes, which was quickly passed over the counter, without a word, by the bookie's wife. I paid for the cigarettes and made my exit. My intention was to make another visit to the shop later when the coast was clear. It had been obvious to me that the strangers were coppers. Later on in the day, I saw Mr. "T" being escorted by the two men, walking past the factory and on their way to Bridewell Police Station. Mr. "T" was duly charged with keeping an illegal book and received a hefty fine. I had my suspicions that the coppers knew what I was up to that day in the shop, but turned a blind eye as I was so young. Lucky me, I got away with it and returned many, many times, to hand over hundred of betting slips in the following three years.

A description of the sticky factory is now appropriate. The factory took in tons of bagged Demerara and white Tate and Lyle sugar. The sugar was boiled up in massive cooking vats, various components such as water, sometimes liquorice, with acid added, depending on what product was being made. But all types of inverted sugar were used in the brewery trade to make beer, stout and ales. To "invert" sugar meant to reduce it to a liquid state and it would not revert back to crystals. The product eventually set to a solid form. The brewery firms bought the invert sugar in liquid, or solid state, from Duttson and Knight Ltd. In liquid, the invert sugar was sold in wooden casks. Solid state invert was sold in cardboard cartons. Whichever type was used there was no fear of the invert reverting back to crystal in the beer.

The factory was large with cellars, a ground floor and three upper floors. The system was as follows.

Sugar came in two-hundredweight bags, but there were some weighing two and a half hundredweights; occasionally, three hundred weight. The lightest bags, if one could call them that, were the Tate and Lyle white sugar at two-hundredweight. The Demerara varied between two, and two and a half hundredweight. The soggiest and heaviest was the Barbados sugar at three-hundredweight. Scammell lorries were used to bring the loads in from Pylle Hill railway sidings. Each load was fifteen tons, the Scammell would back on to the unloading bay in Little Bishop Street the bags were then trucked to the factory door, where the bags were tilted over onto a moving escalator and carried upward through a gap in the next floor up. On the receiving floor was a metal platform where the bags dropped. At shoulder height they were caught and carried away to the stacking line by the men. The stacking system was a work of art. Each bag was carried by one man on his shoulders, then the bag was thrown down to lie atop the bags already lined up on the floor, all the bags would lie flatwise. When the line was three bags high and three lines deep, a system of planks of wood were used to carry the bags up on to the tiers, and stacked to increase the height of bags by another three, and so on. A completed stack of bags would be twenty high and in lines of ten and twenty deep. That would be a high stack of 4,000 bags.

The layout of the factory was used to the best advantage.

The top floor contained the six large steel holding tanks. The bottoms of these tanks were fitted with turn-cocks with steel pipes attached. The pipes descended through to the next floor with a turn-cock and so on down through to the cellars. On each floor was a weighing room. The one immediately below the holding tanks was the carton filling room. The next down was the "pail" filling room, and the cellars were used to fill wood casks with liquid invert sugar. On the other side of the factory were other weighing rooms where the liquid invert sugar, or other products, were filled in to metal drums. The other side of the factory worked on the same principle as the main side, and was supplied with invert sugar from the huge "pan", which boiled tons of sugar every day. Before the mixtures reached the main boiling "pan", they would be put through presses to extract foreign particles, dirt and anything else not required. It was surprising how much waste material was left on the gauze pads of the press after thousands of gallons of liquid had been passed through. The liquid was then pumped up to the "rounds", which were round steel tanks where another part of process took place. The last action was to pump the liquid up into the main boiling "pan".

My Uncle Stan operated and timed the boiling in the main "pan". The "pan" was a massive high, round, steel pot and had viewing port holes to watch the boiling process. It was vacuum sealed. The viewing ports must have had glass inches thick. Once when my Uncle Stan was looking through the port hole, the glass split and Uncle Stan had his face cut. Because the glass had split and the vacuum would had been lost, the "pan" was immediately shut down. When each batch of invert sugar was boiled ready for filling, it was pumped up to the "holding" tanks on the top floor. Each tank would hold approximately twenty five tons of mixture. There were six tanks, so 150 tons could be held in the tanks at any one time. The down pipes through the floors fed each filling point. The first being the carton filling section where one hundred weight of invert was run in to waxed cartons, the carton having been previously placed in a moulding box of wood. Each box was carried away and placed in a line on the floor, which was eventually covered by lines of boxes.

The invert set within three days, depending on the factory temperature, the corners of the boxes were slit down, folded over and secured with a strip of gummed paper. The cartons were then stacked 4X4 on wood pallets, with 4 across the top, making one ton to each pallet. Pallets were taken away and lined up in the loading section on the same floor. The floor below was where metal "pails" were filled with one cwt of invert. A pail was rather like a large metal bucket with a handle each side for carrying. When the pail had received its correct measure of invert, it was carried away by two men, who would place a lid on it, then stack them three high. The invert in the pails normally took to three days to set. When it was set, a sealing wax paper was put into position in each pail to keep the contents clean and the lid was replaced and wired to the handles. The cellars were where the invert was weighed in to the wood casks. Sizes used were barrels, kilos, kegs, and pins. After each cask was filled it was sealed with a wood bung which was hammered in to the bunghole. The factory employed two coopers who kept the filling sections going with casks and they also checked loads going out for leaks. Naturally, because the liquid was sealed, air tight, in the cask it would not set, that is not for weeks anyway. If it did set, then the contents would have to be steamed out of the cask at the brewery. Cartons were loaded on to the lorries by throwing the blocks down a shute. The cartons were slowed-up by means of a wood "brake". Scammells could carry 300 cartons in one load, that equalled 15 tons. The wood casks and metal drums were simply rolled out and loaded on to the Scammells. Pails were trucked out in pairs to the vehicles and "topped-up" in to threes in a line.

My job in the factory was to "make-up" the wood moulds and cartons ready for filling with invert. It was quite simple to do. A carton was hand-stamped with a batch number, checked that it would not leak (repair if necessary), chalk-dust all sides of the carton, then place the carton in to the mould-box. A wood bottom was added to each mould-box. When the cartons of invert had set they were knocked out of the moulds by picking up the mould and then dropping the mould on to an ordinary brick. Some cartons slid out of their moulds with rips in the cardboard; these were sealed over with gummed paper.

# CHAPTER 13

May, 1945 . . . The end of the War in Europe.

I was just sixteen years of age, had put on a bit of weight, but not much, and sprouting up a bit. I was about 5 feet 5 inches tall.

Donald and Joe were soon to be demobbed. My Uncle Wilfred, who also was demobbed, came home to resume work at the Brewer Invert factory.

Uncle Stan's boys, Stanley, Clifford, and Philip also were in the Army, and they returned to work in the factory when they came out of the forces. But, they did not stay long in this job and moved on.

I must go back a few years now to explain an event which took place in 1940. My Uncle Stan was a widower and he married my father's youngest sister, Rose, who therefore was my aunt before and after marriage. Aunt Rose had three boys, twins – Maurice and Bernard – and Trevor, the youngest.

My Aunt Rose died of consumption in 1950. She had worked for years at Wills in Bedminster, where the tobacco dust affected her lungs.

When my brother Donald was in the Army he learned to drive and he got a job with Simmond's brewery, driving and delivering. Joe returned and resumed work with Shattocks.

Mother was still doing a bit of stitching at home. This stopped for a couple of years because Joyce and her family lived at Lockleaze. Joyce and Joe had two children, Georgine, Ivan. When they moved to live in Willinton Road, opposite our house, then Joe started bringing work home again for mother to do.

When Donald came out of the Army he lived at home for a while, but moved away when he married Joyce Coles. Joyce was a member of a family, who like us, were moved out of Hill Street. In later years Donald, Joyce and their young family moved back to live in Knowle.

# CHAPTER 14

April 1947 . . . I received a letter from the services medical board, to attend a medical to assess my fitness for the forces. I was passed A1. In May, when I was eighteen years of age I received my call-up papers, and was instructed to report to Reservoir Camp in Gloucester, for my initial six weeks training. The camp was for training Army recruits, and the primary training was "square-bashing", route marches, physical-training, and rifle shooting on the firing ranges. The term of service, for a conscript, was two years. It was going to be a long haul and I had mixed feelings. But I soon settled down to Army life, and on reflection I enjoyed my two years plus, and would not have missed it for anything. There was some hard slogging but I would have been doing that anyway back in civvy street. On the other hand there were many easy times, and new places to stay in. If I had not been enlisted, I would have never seen the places I did during my Army service.

After the initial training, a number of us squaddies were sent down to the Royal Engineers' barracks at the Verne Citadel in Portland, near Weymouth. The barracks were actually dungeon casemates and partly underground, very gloomy and eerie. It was said that the place was haunted by a headless drummer-boy. The apparition never showed during my time there. The Verne Citadel was, in fact, used to keep French prisoners-of-war at the time of the Napoleonic Wars. Portland would be an island if it was not joined to the mainland by a causeway which carries one road and a single line railway track alongside. From Portland runs a high pebble beach, stretching along the backwaters of Weymouth town right down the coast to Wareham. The Chesil Beach is twenty miles long, and was reckoned to have been thrown up during one night's storm in the early nineteenth century. In places the beach is very high and the size of the pebbles varies from small to some the size of coconuts. At the Verne, we learned all about making knots and hitches, dry land bailey bridging, bomb disposal and the other special skills associated with the Royal Engineers. We also did pontoon bailey bridging on the waters between Chickerell Bank and Chesil Beach. The bank was meadowland. A stretch of water was called the "Fleet" and this flowed in a fast current between the bank and Chesil Beach. Beyond the beach was the open sea. Across the fast flowing current were anchored a dozen or so pontoon boats. A section of bridge would be assembled and laid across to connect two pontoons together. This was repeated all along the line of pontoons until the beach was reached. This was one of the harder tasks, very heavy, and could be dangerous as many heavy metal girders were used. It was summer time and all we wore whilst bridging were shorts, boots and a lifesaver jacket. Everyone, even officers and NCOs, were compelled to wear lifesaving jackets. The fast flowing current was dangerous, too, with undercurrents. There was always a manned motor-boat, ready to rescue anyone in difficulties in the water, during the bridging. After the day's exertions we were taken by truck back to the Verne. Sometimes we stayed at the camp in Chickerell Village. We did our dry-land bailey bridging on a piece of rough waste-land outside of the Verne. The bridge was built in sections and pushed across a deep ravine. The method was to add on a section to act as a counter-balance and then push the first section on "rockers" out across the void. A strict balance was maintained to prevent disaster. Each section added meant one more section to be push out. When we were working on the bridging we had observed, way down in the ravine, some mangled girders etc, and when inquiring as to how they had got there, we were told that a previous squad, had not got the balancing right, so the sections plunged down into the ravine. It must have been too hazardous a job to retrieve the girders and they probably would have been unusable anyway. Those girders are probably still there today. This bridging was extremely hard work also. But as we went into the final job of laying the steel sheet flooring on to the girders we knew the feeling of achievement.

On a really clear day, from the clifftop of the Verne, it is possible to see the faint coastline of the Isle-of-Wight in the far distance.

Our rifle shooting abilities were kept up to scratch by practising on the firing range. We also practised setting up a controlled explosion, by using detonators, primers, slabs of gun cotton and cordex fusewire. We also went mine hunting, using metal detectors. Off duty in the evenings we went into Weymouth by bus, or train, for a drink and a game of darts.

34

Sapper Leon and friend at Officers' Mess, Cambrai
Barracks, Tidworth, 1949.

Leon presented with prize for winning .303 rifle shooting competition at Bomb
Disposal Unit, Headquarters, Horsham, 1952.

Sappers all: waiters, cooks at
Wyke Regis Weymouth, tented
camp, 1948. Leon is second left in
front row.

'Tanks for the memory': Leon at
Bovington Tank Museum, Dorset,
1983.

Pulling in a section of pontoon bridge at Wyke Regis bridging site on Chesil Beach. Sapper Leon Paice is in right hand team, third from end, 1947.

All aboard to cross 'The Fleet' stretch of water, Leon fourth from right.

Now and again we went to the town cinema, but usually it was too warm for that, as it was still summer time. We more often than not, sat out on the sands or the promenade wall.

Our training at the Verne came to an end. There was to be a "passing out" ceremony and bigwigs, families, and members of the public were to attend. The day came and we marched to the tune of "Wings" played by the band of the Royal Engineers. On the rostrum, a high ranking officer took the salute. With him was the Mayor of Weymouth and other dignitaries. After the parade we packed up our gear and placed it in the stores. Then we were off on ten days' leave. We gave a mighty cheer as we left the barracks on our way to Weymouth railway station.

When we returned from leave we read our standing orders. The whole intake were posted to Germany. The intake was split into groups, bound for different camps in Germany. My group of six men were posted to Hamelin, a small town on the river Weser, near Hanover. The town was of the Pied Piper fame. Besides me, the group consisted of William (Bill) Holden, my best mate, Taffy, Geordie, Brummy and a chap from Cheshire. The next morning the men were off by truck to Weymouth Railway station. Barton Stacey transit camp was the destination for all of us. We would all cross over to Germany, then split up to go to our various camps. The Barton Stacey medical officer gave us our jabs.

# CHAPTER 15

A train took us to Harwich where we went aboard a troop-ship. The North Sea was always thought a nasty crossing in the best of weather and our crossing was no different. The crossing took all night to reach the Hook of Holland, and we were all glad to disembark. Some chaps had been seasick. I managed not to be sick as I had taken some advice and stuffed myself with food before sailing. Most chaps were a pale shade of green as they walked down the gang-planks. I felt a little green myself. At the point of disembarkation was the transit camp, and there we received our dinner, those who could face it, that is. We had a few hours' wait before the troop train arrived to take us on to Germany. The transit camp was a massive place, and while we waited for the train a Dutch orchestra played lovely music.

The weather in England was bitterly cold when we left. It was late November windy, frosty and the forerunner of what was to be the worst winter for frost, ice and snow for many years. That was the 1947 winter, and the weather was always worse, to some degree, in Germany. The troop-train arrived and we boarded. We were given packets of sandwiches for the journey, and tea urns were pushed up and down the corridors, at regular intervals. It was expected to be a six or seven hour train journey to Germany. It took the best part of a day, however, about twenty-two hours allowing for stops to disembark groups of men for their different camps and barracks. Our small group of six sappers were destined to Bielefeld. When we arrived at that station we were picked up by truck and taken to the camp to stay overnight, as the truck from Hamelin would not arrive until the following morning at ten o'clock. We did not take it easy, however, for after we had been fed we were taken to the camp's petrol dump, where we had to tidy the place up, and stack up thousands of full petrol cans. Seeing that we were spare bods as well, we were given the "honour" of forming the camp guard for that night. The next morning at reveille the new day guard took over. We had time to wash and brush up, get our breakfast, and wait for the truck to take us on our way to Hamelin. Hamelin is a small town near Hanover and is on the river Weser. We took about four hours to reach there. The barracks were formerly used by the German Army, very spacious, well built and above all, comfortable and well heated. This was much appreciated over the coming couple of months for the weather was getting worse.

There was a large square in the barracks, nice for drill and marching to keep us warm, as the R.S.M. put it. We were now part of 26 Assault Squadron, 32 Engineering Regiment, Royal Engineers. New shoulder flashes and cap badges were issued. A white lanyard was to be part of the uniform now. Our rifles were handed into the armourers and we were issued with Smith and Wesson 45 pistols, plus a holster. The end of the lanyard was fixed to the butt end of the pistol, the other end looped through our right shoulder epaulette. The holster would be on our left waist. We sewed on our own shoulder flashes.

The squadron was equipped with Churchill tanks and other armoured vehicles. The tanks had special attachments fitted to support the movement of other armoured units. Some had a section of bailey bridge built on top of the tank. If there were large gaps in the ground ahead of the tanks, ours would go down into the gap and enable other tanks to cross the gap. Other tanks had a revolving drum, fitted with lengths of metal chain on the front of the tanks. The drums revolved when the tanks were in motion, and the flaying chains struck the ground ahead of the tanks' path. This action would explode any land-mines ahead. The tanks were called flail-tanks. Another special attachment used was an exploding pipe. A six inch diameter hose-pipe was packed with explosives and 'snaked' out on the ground to explode buried mines in the ground ahead. A tank crew consisted of the Commander (an officer or senior N.C.O.), driver, gunner, wireless-operator. All the crew were trained to interchange duties in cases of emergency. We were all expected also to do maintenance and wash down the tanks. I remember one morning in the worst of the winter weather, when we were washing the caked mud from the tracks of the tank, that the water started to freeze as it came out of the hosepipe. It was bitterly cold. This job would normally be done outside the tank 'hangars'. Engine and inside-tank maintenance was always seen to in the 'hangars'. What jobs could not be done were left for a while and we did upkeep and theory in the classroom. There were many small rooms in the main barracks – six chaps to a bedroom – and large washrooms for ablutions. There were recreation rooms and a library. On the top level was a canteen. The camp also had a large N.A.A.F.I. in the grounds. The six of us replacements were all together in the same room.

The weather was getting worse, if that was possible, and Christmas was approaching. When Christmas Eve morning came we assembled on the parade-ground and were told that there would be no normal duties that day, just a short country run. It was not snowing at the time but very cold and there was a couple of feet of snow on the ground. We changed into our P.T. kit and set off on the "little" run. We ran, floundered and struggled and slipped our way over about five miles of open country. When we arrived back at the barracks most men felt half dead. After a rest, a hot shower and then the rest of the day off, we soon recovered.

Christmas morning, there was no reveille bugle, but a clatter out in the corridor and the barrack room door flew open. "Merry Christmas," yelled the R.S.M. as he wheeled in the tea trolley. He gave each man a cup of tea laced with a measure of Steinhager which was a potent German whisky-type drink. The R.S.M. was a Scot-Canadian and a holy terror every day, except at Christmas time. Even the officers seemed to regard him in awe.

Standing orders were the daily notices posted on the barrack's notice board. Anything to do with the day's business would be displayed there for all to read. Coming events would also be notified to the men. If ever there was one thing not to forget, it was to read "standing orders" daily. Failing to read them meant trouble, real trouble. This is where sappers learned that they were due for guard duty. The date would be given and the named sappers had time to prepare for the night's guard duty. They would normally finish their ordinary duties early in the afternoon, clean and polish their gear, shine their brasses, press their uniforms and have a haircut even if they did not need one. My turn came for a guard duty, so I got pressing and polishing. I had my hair cut although I did not need it. The day-time guard was taken over by the night-time guard in a parade outside the guardroom, at 4 o'clock each afternoon. An officer and the R.S.M. regularly inspected each afternoon's changing of the guard.

For my spell of duty I lined up for inspection with the other five men outside the guardroom. The officer and R.S.M. walked slowly along the line in front of us, not a word spoken, and the inspecting pair then walked along behind the line of men. When the R.S.M. reached the back of my head he bellowed out "and what's your name sapper?" "Paice, Sir" I said. "Well Paice," he bellowed, "if you do not get your hair cut smartish, I'll have you 'pacing' around the square." Very nice, I thought, as I had my hair cut just two hours previously. Was the R.S.M. having a little joke at my expense? Maybe, he could have been.

To get off guard duty, a cast-iron excuse was required and probably also required was a note from the Unit Medical Officer. By the time March arrived the winter was behind us and we were out again with the tanks, getting fully active, exploring the German countryside during our manoeuvres.

There was another duty that sappers were selected for and that was "operation spiv". An officer and ten sappers could be called out at a few minutes' notice to go out on this operation. It did not apply during the day when on normal duties, but in the evenings when off duty. The group of men went out, in a truck, on to the roads, stopping vehicles and questioning the occupants as to their reasons for being on the road. The vehicles were searched for contraband and "black market" goods, which would be confiscated and taken to the German police station. Some of the squaddies bartered their cigarette rations for watches, cameras etc. Twenty cigs plus a small tin of coffee could be, and often was, exchanged for a decent camera. The Germans would also exchange their valuables – gold and silver rings, and brooches – for a packet of cigs. Tobacco and coffee were highly prized by the Germans, which could be exchanged on their "black market" for food, or for money. I must confess that I did an exchange – just the once – and that was for an antique silver ring, but one morning whilst I was washing in the ablutions I left the ring on the ledge of the washing basin. When I realized that I had forgotten to put it back on my finger, I returned to the washroom. The ring was gone and I never found out who had taken it.

Although I had done a fair amount of driving as a member of a tank crew, I and five other sappers were sent on a "top-up" driving course with the 2nd. Royal Tank Regiment based at the School of Infantry, Warminster, Nr. Salisbury. It was the middle of March, a lovely Spring morning. We took just our small back-packs, personal side-weapons, which we were solely responsible for, and these were Smith & Wessons revolvers, plus personal kit for washing and shaving etc. The course was of six weeks duration. We were split in to two trios, each having a R.T.R.

41

Sergeant instructor. My instructor was Sergeant Hanks, a very pleasant man and what he taught us about tank driving and maintenance could not have been bettered.

So, after the long tedious trip back from Germany over the same tiresome route, we were back in England. The beauty of it was that after the end of training each Friday at about four-thirty pm, we were given week-end passes and had until first parade at eight-thirty am on Monday to report back at camp. This meant that I was home about six-thirty each Friday evening, for a long week-end, as Warminster was only about a hour's train ride from Bristol. I caught the "milk train" at five-thirty from Temple Meads station on the Monday mornings to get back to Warminster. It was slow but gave me enough time to get back for the eight-thirty parade.

On our first night at the camp we were given the honour of doing the camp guard and fire patrol duty, wouldn't you know it? For our driving hours we took a tank along to the nearby Imber ranges, taking turns at the controls. We took grub with us and stayed all day driving on various ground conditions. Some of the terrain was pretty rough but we had a great time dropping over deep ditches and climbing the opposite gradients. For brief moments it was like shooting up into thin air, and then a tremendous drop back to earth and downwards. There was flat ground but also plenty of dips and steep banks. A great time was had by all.

The six weeks soon passed and we were on our way back to Germany and our barracks in Hamelin. That journey, again. We arrived back on the Saturday morning. The first thing we did on arrival was to read "standing orders". We were amazed to read that the Squadron were in the throes of packing, because the following Monday the Squadron were off back to England. So we had the weekend to get our stuff up together and think of "that journey" again. We were hoping that it would be the last time, and as it turned out, it was. A dozen or so men would remain to drive the tanks and trucks to the German port ready for shipping back to England. That operation would take a while and our "hardware" was expected to reach our new camp in a month. We collected our kitbags from the stores and generally got ready for Monday morning. The morning came and the troops were off. Marching through the town (with no Pied Piper) we reached the local railway station where a troop-train took the squadron all the way to the Hook of Holland. The usual ship took us over the North Sea to Harwich. A train then took us to Salisbury, where we boarded trucks which took us to our new home at Tidworth – Cambrai barracks it was – about ten miles from Salisbury. We spent a couple of days getting ourselves sorted, then went on ten days' disembarkation leave. The real work started on our return from leave.

42

There was much to do in the way of repairs, painting and getting the camp up to scratch. The camp had some hangars which needed attention before our tanks could be housed in them. The camp was used by the American forces during the war and other units of the British army since then. It was an extensive camp having two lots of barracks. There was a large canteen run by the N.A.A.F.I. and a larger still cookhouse, plus a recreation room. We had a library and gymnasium. The barracks were brick-built and comfortable on two levels. There were some huts but only used occasionally as overspills. So we spent a couple of months on the tidying up process, mending and painting. To break the monotony we also did square bashing and arms drill. All was prepared and ready when the tanks and other vehicles arrived. The squadron was now back up to strength.

# CHAPTER 16

May 1948 . . . Standing Orders: "A" Troop, 26 Squadron will assemble, with small kit, at the Company Office on Monday the 20th May.

That was the message for my troop and we wondered where we were off to this time. The hundred and so men were transported down to Weymouth by trucks and to a familiar place: the bridging camp at Chickerell, near Chesil Beach. We thought "Oh yes", we had an idea what was in store for us. A training scheme had been started for bridging courses and officers and Senior N.C.Os. would attend the course for one week. What was to happen? The trainees built a bailey bridge in the course of a week and the sappers, us, would disassemble the bridge at the end of each course. There was a new intake of trainees every ten days, seven days for "them" to build one and two days for "us" to take it down. The complete body of men, including officers, were under canvas in the meadow side of the bank.

A huge marquee was used as a mess for the officers, there was a wood hut as a cookhouse. The officers slept two to a small tent, sappers were more cramped than that at six to a small tent.

There was a cookhouse for the men at the far end of the meadow, well away from the lines of tents. Word got around that the officers needed mess waiters and so three of us who were well and truly fed up with bridging applied for the jobs. Not only would it be a more "cushy" job but we knew that the waiters had the same meals as the officers, which would usually be after the officers had dined. The three of us got the waiters' jobs and we reported to the mess sergeant. We were fitted out with white jackets and given instruction in the art of table waiting. Although the mess was in a marquee it was properly laid out, long tables and tablecloths with all the knives, forks, spoons, water jugs and wine glasses, flowers etc. The officers had six-course meals, hors d'oeuvres, soup, fish, main course, pudding and savoury, finished off with cheese biscuits and coffee.

There were thirty trainees in one intake, and the three waiters were kept busy during the dining period. The plates of food were carried from the cookhouse across to the marquee. At first we were a bit dodgy about carrying more than two plates at a time but practice makes perfect and we could, after a short while, manage six plates of food at one go, by using all our fingers and thumbs, balancing the plates in conjunction with our wrists. The waiters could get eighteen plates into the dining area in one 'run' from the cookhouse. It was a hectic hour scurrying to and fro' from the cookhouse doing our balancing act. We then cleared up the tables, and reset them ready for breakfast the following morning. Afterwards we took our meal and relaxed for the rest of the evening, possibly going into Weymouth, about fifteen minute walk away, or just stayed in the Bridging Camp. The officers' dinner was at eight o'clock each evening, so by the time we had cleared-up it was getting on for nine fifteen and hardly worth going into town. We did this job for two months and although there was the hectic hour or so each evening, it was better than slogging away taking down and dismantling bridges. There was the bonus of having the same food as the officers too. Lovely grub . . .

August. The last batch of trainees had passed through and the bridges were dismantled for the last time. The officers had gone back to their various camps and our troop of sappers went back to Cambrai barracks at Tidworth. While we were away the other three troops had also been sent off on various tasks. One troop went potato lifting for some hard-pressed farmers in Sussex. I would not have fancied that job. The lads were well supplied with cider, however.

I had really taken to the mess waiter job so, when I heard that there was a vacancy in the officers' mess, I applied for and got it. It meant leaving the barrack-room and moving in to the officers' building, where the waiters and batmen were quartered in a small wing of the building. The building had small bedrooms for each officer and on one floor there were a dozen rooms, which housed two to three sappers to each room. There were four waiters and ten batmen who looked after all the officers. There were two cooks, a barman, and a Sergeant in charge. There was a long dining room, and the dining table was placed in the centre of the room and was nearly the length of the dining room. Connected to the dining room was an ante-room.

Both rooms had plush carpets, walls were oak panelled. There were side tables in the dining room. Long drapes hung from the windows. At the far end of the dining room was a large table on which was displayed the Squadron's trophies and silver. On the wall hung the regimental colours and crossed paddles completed the display.

It was possible to seat forty officers at the table, but I never witnessed a full sitting as most of the time, officers were away on courses, or commanding the spud lifters or something like that. When I was a permanent mess waiter I had nothing to do with the tanks any more and I saw much less of my old mates, including Bill Holden. As well as waiting duties the four of us had the responsibility of polishing the furniture and tables, the oak panelling, vacuuming the carpets, cleaning windows and polishing the silver.

After each night's dinner we had our meal in the cookhouse and then helped with the washing up. After the washing up, the dining table would be reset and laid out for the following morning's breakfast. The ante-room would need clearing up because that was where the officers took their after-dinner coffee. Coffee was never served at the dining table. When officers were present in the camp, tea and coffee breaks were always served in the ante-room. Dinner was at the usual time of eight in the evenings. At times, visiting officers stayed to dinner. We had two officers from the Irish Republic staying at the mess who were on a course.

Also we had a new officer posted to our Squadron. Capt. John Barker R.E. was an extremely likeable man who got on well with his fellow officers and men in the ranks. He was popularly known as Gentleman John Barker by all in the camp.

It was Spring 1949 and the former troop that I was in were sent to a bridging camp in Sussex, to a similar set-up as was in Chickerell in Dorset. Again it was for the training of officers in bailey bridging. Part of another of our troops of men also went, six officers and several N.C.Os., plus three batmen and three mess waiters including me. The training ground was near Blackwater in Sussex, but I cannot remember the name of the camp. The mess waiters joined in with the others on duty at the officers' mess. The camp was set in some lovely countryside. Our living quarters were nissen huts close to the cookhouse. Most days, meals were taken to the bridging site for the officers and sappers, the site being some twenty minutes' truck drive away.

It was at Blackwater Camp that Capt. John Barker got a group of us interested in photography and processing films for printing. Most of us had a camera and the surrounding countryside was the ideal spot for taking photographs. When we wanted our films processed and printed we would have to go in to town for them to be done. Then perhaps, have to wait for a week to fetch the finished prints. Capt. John used to do his own developing and enlarging in a spare hut in the camp. He had all the equipment including an enlarger, and spent a good deal of his free time working on his hobby. It was Capt. John's idea to start a class in photography and processing. About fifteen sappers enrolled with him and we all chipped in to buy the necessary chemicals and photographic printing paper. We received expert tuition from Capt. John and were soon developing and printing our own films. We were all highly delighted with the results. Hundreds of films were processed and printed, which in the long run, saved money as well. Capt. John gave me a large enlargement of a photograph of his aunt's cottage somewhere in Surrey. I have that photograph to this day.

The troop of men returned to Cambrai Barracks in mid-June, and I had a couple of weeks' service to do before my demob. My release No. was 111. A special notice was posted on Standing Orders one morning to the effect that all National Service conscripts would be required to serve an extra three months. That meant that I still had just over three months' service to do. Que sera sera. I think the extended service was due to the current situation in Suez, and some other trouble spots in the Middle East and throughout the world . . . Life went on, in Cambrai and elsewhere. The mess waiters and the batmen were excused from doing guard-duty but there was a roster for all the mess staff to do a turn as duty batman. This involved manning the officers' mess telephone all night in the duty room and perhaps pressing the odd uniform, polishing buttons, for the officers whose regular batman was on leave.

I was duty batman one night when the phone rang, to be told "the N.A.A.F.I. is on fire, quick, get the duty officer down here." Normally the duty officer would stay up to about midnight, then if all was quiet, he would retire to bed. This particular night, I thought Capt. Gaiger was the duty officer, so off I dashed up the stairs to Capt. Gaiger's bedroom, to awaken him and pass on the message. "Right," said Capt. Gaiger, "I'll be down in a jiffy." I returned to the duty room. The night moved on. Was my face red the following morning when I learned that Capt. Gaiger was not the duty officer for the previous night. In fact, Capt. John Barker was, but nothing was made of it and after a little leg-pulling, it was soon forgotten. The weeks were steadily passing by, all the men were now back from the various out-posts and farms. The Squadron had a new posting and most of the officers, including Capts. John Barker and Gaiger were off to Hong Kong. Quite a number of my old mates were going too, including a few who "signed on" for seven years just to go abroad to Hong Kong. Bill Holden was not one of them to sign on.

Bill and I had the same release No. 111, and had a couple of weeks to go before our release. Bill could not wait to get out of the Army. I had mixed feelings about it. I think I was starting to get bored with my Army life and wanted to go home to see what was happening there. The notice appeared on the board. "Release group No.111. Sappers with this group No. will be released from service on Monday 18th August. They will report to the guardroom at 9am. for transport to Ludgershall railway station where a train will take personel to the Aldershot demobolising centre. In the meantime, all kit, weapons, are to be handed in to the stores. Uniforms will be retained and handed in to the stores at Aldershot, when personel have changed in to their civvies. Clearance chits will be required from all stores and the Library etc, before your departure on Monday. All personnel will report to the Commanding Officer's office at 4pm, on Friday 13th August, for a farewell talk."

We had all done the various things with the stores by mid-day on Saturday. All we retained was the uniform for the time being, and our bedding and eating tools. These were to be handed in on our last morning in the camp. Saturday evening a group of us went in to Salisbury for a farewell drink. Sunday we lazed around in the morning and went to the cinema in Tidworth in the evening. After the film show we walked back to the barracks recounting our days in the Army. The morning dawned. This was it. Monday 18th August, 1949 . . .

I cannot remember anyone bothering about getting breakfast. I know I did not. We hurriedly got washed and shaved, handed in our bedding and eating tools, said cheerio to the few officers and men still in the mess and made our way to the guardroom. Naturally we were a little early, by about twenty minutes. While we were waiting by the guardroom the C.S.M. came along and stopped to say farewell, wishing us all the best, as he shook each man's hand. The truck arrived and we were off. I looked out the back of the truck as we went out of the gates. The truck sped away from the camp and I watched as my Army days were now to be part of the past. The final step. Aldershot, we handed in our uniform, got documented, received our railway passes for the station to catch our trains home.

Bill Holden, Gadd and Venables caught a train for London. Another chap caught a train to somewhere else, while I waited a little longer for a train to Ash. From Ash I caught a train to Three Bridges, then another train to Reading, where I then caught a train to Bristol. It must have been mid-afternoon when I arrived at Temple Meads, got a bus to Melvin Square, a little walk then I was home, a civilian again . . . I thought that I would probably not ever see Bill Holden again. He did not keep in touch. I received a Christmas card that year from Capt. John Barker who was in Hong Kong. He asked me how I was getting on in Civvy Street and was it living up to expectations? I replied to the card but unfortunately I never heard from the Capt. again. He had

47

mentioned on his card that my mates who had gone with him to Hong Kong were having a wonderful time. I often wonder if Capt. Gentleman John Barker is still alive and where he lives in England. Perhaps, he now lives in the lovely little cottage in Surrey, I wonder. At the time I knew him he was, I should think about thirty five years old. He would be around 80 years now.

# CHAPTER 17

1949. Civvy Street. I had a week off, staying at home but started work at Duttsons the following Monday. I was too old to be a teaboy so I went as a driver's mate on one of the Scammells. I worked in the factory also a lot of the time. The driver's name was Ted Sage, a very nice chap. We made journeys to and fro, from the railway siding at Pylle Hill, to fetch bags of Tate and Lyle sugar, 150 bags at a time, 15 tons.

We man-handled the bags out of the railway trucks and stacked them on the Scammell. Each load was taken back to the factory and off-loaded by using a pair of hand trucks, to wheel the bags to the bottom of the moving escalator. The escalator carried the bags upwards to the next floor. There the bags were stacked close to the boiling vat. I should explain here that the bags were really sacks, of course. Why the factory hands always called them bags, I never did learn. When there was to be a boiling session, the bags were wheeled to the vat and lifted on to a wood platform; the bag would be opened by undoing the stitching, and then lifted and tilted over the edge of the vat so emptying the contents in to the vat. The sugar with other ingredients was then boiled for a certain length of time, then passed through filters which were situated in the "press". The filters were giant frames covered with canvas cloth, there were 40 of these frames within the "press" and when a batch of sugar was being passed through, the whole lot of the frames were squeezed together to make one solid block. The squeezing was achieved by turning a giant screw mechanism. It was surprising just how much 'debris' was extracted from each batch by the filtering action. When a batch was finished the screw mechanism was released so that the frames could be separated and then the caked 'debris' washed away. After this had been done the frames were reset with canvas cloth and re-squeezed by the screw, ready for the next batch. From the "press" room the filtered syrup was then pumped up to the boiling "Pan", which was on the next floor. Uncle Stan then operated the "Pan" to give the syrup its final boiling. When the batch was ready, it was then pumped up to the "holding" tanks, on the top floor. The liquid was tapped off, in to the various containers on each floor, usually the following day. It could wait in the tanks for several days though.

My brother Donald and his mate, John Milton, sometimes drove into the factory to pick up a load of casks of Invert for Simmonds Brewery. John Milton is known as Milton John, the actor.

I was courting Joan Wheadon, who lived in Creswicke Road, and we became engaged in 1950. We were married at St. Barnabas Church, Knowle, on 28.7.1951.

There were now spare rooms at our house in Willinton as my sister Joyce, and my brother Donald were married and living in their own houses, elsewhere in Bristol. Joan and I had the parlour room as a living room, and the medium size bedroom. Not long after Joan and I married, my sister Joyce and her family moved back to Willinton and lived opposite us. The same thing happened with Donald's family. They moved back to Willinton to live next door to my sister Joyce. With Joe living on our doorstep it was very convenient to bring home stitching work for my mother and Joyce, who did the work in our house at 110.

Donald had left Simmonds Brewery and was now working for Radio Rentals, as a radio/tv engineer. He was self-taught in this new work.

Vernon had taken a job with the Bristol Corporation maintenance dept. Dion had completed his national service in the Royal Navy, and was now home and working for Wills tobacco in Bedminster.

Joan was expecting a baby in the coming May. When her time drew near, the doctors had her in early because of high blood pressure. Joan was in Mortimer House Maternity Hospital two weeks before the birth of the baby, and two weeks after, because of the blood pressure.

Denise was born on 30.5.1952. Joan had signed herself out of the hospital, and her mother Ivy went to fetch her and the new baby home to Willinton Road.

The next to be married was Dion and he married Margaret Longman, who lived at the bottom of Willinton Road. Margaret was an only child. When Dion and Margaret were married they lived in with Margaret's parents. Denise had been baptised at St. Barnabas Church in Knowle.

My sister Joyce looked after Denise while Joan worked at the Cabin up at Filwood. I had become an uncle many times over.

Joyce and Joe had three children Georgine, Josephine, and Ivan.

Donald and his wife Joyce had four children, Richard, Lee, Robert, and Neil.

Dion and Margaret had two daughters, Paula and Bernice.

Vernon was the last to marry and married a divorcee with two sons. His wife's name was June, the sons being Martin and Adrian.

Vernon and June's only child was Keith.

49

Dion and Joyce at back, with Margaret Longman and Leon's mother, Doris, 1950.

Brother Donald and wife Joyce, 1947.

Leon 1947 aged 18 years.

Brother Dion, 1948 aged 17 years.

Leon's wedding day, July 28th, 1951 with brothers Vernon, left and Donald.

51

The happy couple:
Leon and Joan at St
Barnabas Church,
Knowle. July 28th,
1951.

Joan at Whitchurch Airport display, c.1954.

# CHAPTER 18

Another situation had arisen in the Middle East in July 1952.

Reservists were being called up to do a fortnight's retraining in the forces. I was an "X" reservist and although it only applied to National Service, not to the regular army, there were a number of men who had been in the forces as National Service men 1946–1948 who were called up for the training. The camp, an engineers', was in Horsham, Sussex.

Denise was only two months old and I thought "what a time to be away from home!" At the camp we did the usual training: bridging, bomb disposal and weapon shooting on the firing range. There were a few hundred men at the camp and everyone, including officers and N.C.O.s, had to use a rifle and fire five rounds at targets on the firing range.

We used 303 rifles and points scored were four points for a 'bull' three points for an 'inner' and two points for an 'outer'.

Another sapper and myself were the only ones to score a maximum. We shot again for the decider. My opponent shot a maximum again, but I got 2 points less. When the fortnight's training was finished we had a parade, and prizes were given to competition winners.

A Brigadier took the salute and presented the prizes on the parade ground. There were 1st and 2nd Prizes in all the events. Yours truly received his prize for runner-up in the shooting competition, and photographs were taken of the event. Needless to say, I have copies of those photographs. A job which we enjoyed doing at Horsham was blowing stumps of trees out of the ground for the farmers. The farmers would cut the trees down to ground level and we were invited by the farmers, to fix explosives below the tree's ground level, detonate, and so blow the stump out of the ground. It was good practice in the art of preparation for a controlled explosion. There was a strict rule for anyone dealing with explosives. This was always complied with, without fail. It was to place the charge correctly, using the correct amount of explosive, to prime the charge correctly by using the correct length of fuse and never, never, turn and run when the fuse had been lit. The reason for this rule being that if the man lighting the fuse ran he could fall, stumble or trip over an obstacle on the ground and stun himself, perhaps lose consciousness. That would have been very dangerous with the explosion imminent.

Readers will remember that earlier, I wondered if I would ever see Bill Holden again. Well, I did. For one of the first persons I met on arrival at the camp was Bill and we were soon talking of the old days. As it was, there were a few other men at the camp that I knew from earlier Army days.

The weather had been extremely hot and sticky, our last night at the camp finished with a violent thunderstorm. I thought of Joan at home, with our little baby. Joan was not too keen on thunderstorms, but would have had the other family members there. The following day we left the camp to return home.

January. 1953. Father was losing weight and feeling ill. He kept working as long as he could. He was now working at George's Brewery because Simmonds had closed down. It got to a point where he was too weak to work. Our doctor did not know what was wrong with him. Eventually it was decided to send him for tests. First he was taken to Southmead Hospital, where they could not find out what was wrong. He was then taken to the Bristol Royal Infirmary where he was diagnosed as having cancer of the throat. Father was brought home and my mother was told that he had just three months to live. The growth in his oesophagus would prevent him from eating and he would literally starve to death. Everyone was devastated by the terrible news. As father steadily grew weaker and weaker, thinner, and looking like a living skeleton, he took to his bed. He had but a few weeks left and I was so worried and upset, that I couldn't go to work. I stayed home with him. I stayed in the bedroom and watched over him, I couldn't do anything else. He was so weak, he could hardly whisper. Sometimes he lifted his hand as he saw me in the room and he tried to speak but the words always faded on his lips. I used to hold his hand and wish it was all over for him, but he suffered on. One afternoon near the end of his life, I was surprised to hear him whispering as there had been no sound from him for some days. I moved up closer. He was facing the wall and feebly pointed to the wall. I got really close to try and catch what he was saying. His words were not very clear, but I would swear that he said "who's that little boy standing over there?" Did he see the spirit of his little boy Keith who had died so very, very young? That night I said a prayer for God to end my father's suffering. The following morning we were awakened by a knock on our bedroom door. It was my mother and she said that my father had passed away in the night. Can things be imagined when a person is very worried and all keyed up? I do not know. Maybe things do happen in times of crisis and are very real.

Something else happened besides the "little boy in the bedroom" and I relate this here. I was sitting in our room opposite the foot of the stairs, the door open so that I could listen out for father. On this particular afternoon, all was quiet and father was asleep upstairs. I was the only other person in the house at the time. I was looking at a newspaper when

I heard a slight swishing sound coming from the stairs, I looked up and saw a figure of a person gliding down the stairs. The figure looked like an old lady dressed in a long flowing purple gown. When it reached the bottom of the stairs, it turned past the open door of the room I was sitting in and gave a silent little glance at me as it passed through the hallway to disappear out of sight. If I was nodding off, then I was dreaming, or awake, my imagination running riot, but I believe that I really did see the ghostly figure and that it was an ancestor, from hundreds of years ago.

My father was buried in the same grave as little Keith at Greenbank Cemetery. Father was sixty years old.

Joan worked for Horlers at the Cabin sweetshop. Denise was still in the charge of my sister Joyce during the daytime. In between times, mother and Joyce did stitching in the living room at 110 Willinton Road.

I did not return to work at the Brewers Invert factory after the death of my father. Instead, I commenced work for a motor factors store in Victoria Street. The work involved loading, packing post parcels, stocking the store shelves, unloading goods from the main store which were brought by lorry, and stocktaking. The shelves were stacked with all manner of motor parts such as pistons, gaskets, valves, valve springs, cylinder liners, piston rings and gudgeon pins. The main stock check was done annually. It was done after closing hours and for about four hours each evening of a week. I stayed in this job for seven years. It was not interesting work really, but well paid and secure.

In 1960 I was fed up with the piston trade and moved on. I landed up working for Goodyear Tyres in Temple Way. It was stores again but a little more interesting than my former job. My job was in the stores loading and off-loading all sizes of tyres. I also was the tyre examiner for remoulds. Loads of tyres were brought in for examination for me to assess their worthiness for remoulding. Some would be entirely scrapped because they were too worn for a remould. Others worth remoulding were documented by size, customer etc, and then sent down to the remoulding factory in Winterstoke Road. When the tyres were returned to the Temple Way store en-bloc, they were sorted for collection by the customers. The customers would not receive their own tyres back, but the same quantity, by size, as they had submitted.

It was now 1961, and I was 32 years of age, Joan 30, Denise 8. We were now living in a flat in Hareclive Road, Hartcliffe. Joan was working in a Sweetshop in Symes Avenue. Denise was attending Hareclive Junior school. A few years on and Denise was attending the Bishport Seniors. That was the time when it became the fashion for school-kids to have recorders. It was also the new fashion for the kids to play their recorders in school and when the tune 'Telstar' hit the charts, most kids could play it quite well. It was about the only tune that Denise could play well. The kids must have had plenty of practice on that tune.

Joan's mother, Ivy Victoria had been a stage performer for quite a number of years prior to marriage and was a very good dancer. Joan would have liked to have followed in her mother's footsteps, to sing and dance, but was too shy. We tried to get Denise interested in dancing but she lacked the interest, and she gave up after two lessons in tap-dancing. There was an art teacher at Bishport School named John Paice, and I wondered whether he was a relative of mine as he also had ancestors from the Isle of Wight. John collected his morning paper from the shop where Joan worked, and Joan mentioned to him that my family came from the island. Joan also mentioned my interest in family history, and that I would like to meet him. John agreed that there were strong possibilities of a link between our two families, and looked forward to a chat regarding this. Unfortunately, I lingered a while before thinking of arranging a meeting and left it too late, for John Paice had left the school and was working elsewhere. Some cartoons by a John Paice were appearing in the Bristol newspaper, *The Western Daily Press*, at times at a later date. This must have been the same person.

When we lived in the masionnette in Hareclive Road, we would watch the work going on alongside the row of shops in Symes Avenue. Piledrivers were being used to get firm foundations for the high-rise flats and the excavations were pretty deep.

Our next door neighbour, Alfie worked on the site and when some fossils were found he gave Denise four. The grey stones were oval shaped and weighed approximately two pound each. The stones had a criss-cross pattern of cracks in them. The cracks sparkled with some brown crystals entrapped within. The cracks were on the tops of the stones, the undersides being smooth.

One Saturday morning Denise and I went up to the City Museum and took one of the stones with us. We asked to see someone. The expert on geology was not there, so we left the stone and our address with a member of the staff. A few days later, a letter arrived to explain what the stone was. It was a "Septarian Noodle" formed millions of years ago in the "Lower Lias" layer of the Earth's formation. The "Noodle" had formed in the mud-bed of a river which had dried up, the stone had cracked across its surface and rain percolating down through the earth had deposited the minerals in the stone's cracks, which in time formed the crystals. The curator was so interested in the "Noodle" that he asked if we could spare one for the display at the Museum. The following Saturday we returned to the Museum and gave the curator the largest of the four stones. Denise took one stone to school which was placed in the school's display collection. I still have the other two stones. One of these has a fossilised moth on its underside, partly imbedded in the stone.

# CHAPTER 19

Photography took up much of my spare time. I was using a good type of 35mm camera and processing some films as well. I had an enlarger and "blew up" many shots. At the time of writing, I have thirty or so albums crammed with thousands of photographs. Black and white, and colour, of all sizes. My collection contains hundreds of colour transparencies also. Colour photography was pretty expensive in the early days. A colour film could cost as much as twenty shillings and the processing about ten shillings. This was, of course, shop processing. Prints were available, but again pretty expensive at four shillings each. That was for a two by two inch print. Transparencies did not cost as much, they were returned already mounted in cardboard or plastic mounts ready for viewing, but this of course required a projector, and a screen. Most of my colour prints and transparencies were taken when on holiday or visits to special places such as cathedrals and abbeys. I purchased *The Amateur Photographer* each month. In this publication I spotted an advertisement for the sale of a discontinued colour film. It was Dufaycolor 35mm transparency film. The film was slightly outdated stock in tins of 100 feet, at two pounds five shillings per tin. I had used the film previously and it was an amazingly good colour transparency film, giving true-to-life colours. The film was thicker than normal because it incorporated three filters: red, yellow, blue and they gave a particularly good colour balance when exposed. I think the film's thickness and the introduction of competitive, quick processing and thinner, cheaper films brought about Dufaycolor's demise. Also, whereas previously films had to be paid for to have them developed, the newer ones were sold "process paid". They would be processed, and posted back, ready mounted and ready for viewing.

A 'still' projector was now part of my equipment and I also bought a screen. So I decided to purchase a tin of the Dufay film. Although the film was going off the market, a laboratory was still in business and willing to process the films. The charge was five shillings per 24-exposure film.

I had planned that I would cut the bulk length of film into 24 exposure strips. This would be thirty-three films. Each length of twenty-four exposure film measured three feet so that meant that thirty-three films could be obtained from the 100 feet bulk film. They would not be returned mounted however, which meant purchasing a box of cardboard mounts at about five shillings. There were 100 mounts to a box. That was no problem; the main thing was cutting the film and loading it into the individual cassettes. I gave this some thought, as the film would have to be handled in total darkness. What I did was to measure a length of string against an old 24 exposure film that I had, and knotted the string to the appropriate length, approximately 3 feet. The next thing I needed to do was get hold of some empty film cassettes. I went down town to a photographic shop where developing was done and enquired if they had some empty cassettes to spare, whereupon I was given a box full of a hundred or so "empties" free of charge. I think the "empties" usually ended up in the ashbin.

Now I was ready to start work on loading the cassettes. I worked in a darkened room with my piece of string and a pair of scissors handy. I had previously taken the tops off the cassettes and loosened all tins etc. First I opened the bulk tin of film and then measured my knotted piece of string against it. I cut at the appropriate knot, then wound the short piece of film on to the spool of the cassette and then placed the loaded spool in to its drum and put the cover top back onto the cassette. I repeated this operation until I had finished the bulk film off. I had 34 films from the bulk length. These lasted me a considerable time. Of course, I could not go mad and shoot off film after film as there was still the processing charge but eventually I used up all the film, and as I have already written, have many hundreds of excellent Dufaycolor transparencies. It wasn't long before I got the Cine-bug. I had the urge to film persons in motion. I had a little stroke of money luck, so I bought a Bell-Howell 8mm, cine-camera. It was of course a silent movie camera. It used a 25 foot roll of film, 16mm. The film was run through the camera and then reversed to run through again. The film would have been exposed on one side, for the total length and again when reversed it would have been exposed on the other side. When the film was processed it would have been split right along the middle and then spliced together to make one 50 foot length of film. Each 50 foot film lasted only 4 minutes on the cine projector. Films could, of course, be spliced together to make 100, 150, 200, and so on up to 600 foot. Most home projectors were for up to 600 foot anyway. I already had a white screen but now needed a cine projector to show my movie films on. A while later I got the cine projector and it was marvellous to sit and view the cine films taken at home and when we were in various holiday resorts. The cine camera was used to record the marriage of our daughter Denise.

In later years video cameras were taking over from cine camera. I bought a video camera and we always took it on our holidays. Then video firms started transferring cine films to video-tape, which was a good idea as it was more convenient to simply put the tape in to the video machine. It saved having to get out and put up the projector and screen.

I sold my cine projector, and bought a video camera. The cine camera I still have. I kept the screen for showing my colour transparencies. My cine films were silent ones, but when the transfers to video tape were done, music was added with appropriate titling. In between times, I carried on with my other hobbies of stamps, coin collecting, first day covers, reading and my favourite pastime, genealogy. I have been a member of the B.A.F.H.S. in the past. At the moment I am a member of the Hampshire Genealogical Society, The Hampshire Archives Trust, and the Isle-of-Wight Family History Society.

## CHAPTER 20

By 1962 all the family of Paices were married and living in various parts of the city.

Mother lived on her own in Willinton Road. Donald and family had moved from Willinton Road to live in Somerdale Avenue. Joyce and family were still living opposite mother in Willinton Road, but not for long, for they moved out to follow Donald and live in a house next door to him, in Somerdale Avenue.

Dion and Margaret were living in Hartcliffe, with their small daughters but they too eventually moved back to Knowle Park in Wellgarth Walk. Vernon was married to June and living in a prefab at Plummers Hill in St. George.

I was now working for the Cooperative Wholesale Society in the grocery warehouse in Prince Street. My brother-in-law, Royston Wheadon worked there also. It was very hard work but I can honestly say that it was my happiest place of work. There was comradeship and humour, some good laughs, and plenty of little perks. Sid Rust was in charge of a section; I was his side-kick and we got on famously. It was nothing to arrive in the morning and see 15 lorries, laden with tinned fruit or tinned tomatoes waiting to be unloaded. The warehouse handled all manner of grocery goods. Tinned everything, cheese, eggs, sweets, chocolates, oats, fish, tinned meats of all descriptions. Ribena, Lucozade, and much more.

They smoked bacon there. Loads of "green" as we called it, was sent out to various shops in Bristol even down as far as Plymouth. In the smoking room, "green" sides of bacon were carried into the room and hung up on hooks along bars set in the ceiling. The doors were shut tight and smoke fed in to the room. The smoke was produced by burning oak sawdust in the cellar, below the room where the "green" sides were hanging. It took two days of smoking before the bacon was "done". A rota was operated whereby all the warehouse staff took a turn in the smoking room. It was for one day only and a turn was about every three weeks. On that one day, besides carrying bacon into the smoking-room, lorries were off-loaded with bales of "green" sides. A bale was four sides wrapped up and stitched into a wrapper of sacking. The bales were pulled off the lorries, stacked on wood pallets, and then wheeled in to the freezing rooms. The worst part of the "stove" job was carrying the green sides into the stoves for smoking. Although we wore protective clothing the bacon juice still managed to find its way underneath and run down our necks. The "stove" job, especially unloading the lorries, was particularly nasty in winter.

There was a railway line alongside the warehouse, and thousands of tons of goods were taken in through the warehouse windows. There might be a string of four trucks on the line outside the warehouse, with loads of boxes of tinned pears, peaches and some other fruits.

The frames of the windows were slipped out and the roller tracks were passed through the window spaces, from the rail trucks into the warehouse. Two men were inside the truck, and they kept the rollers moving consistently with boxes, which were caught at the warehouse end by a team of men who would stack the boxes six high, and then wheel the stack up elsewhere on the warehouse floor. Sweets and chocolate came by rail too. Most of the fish, like tins of salmon, came by rail too.

I moved on to another job in October 1964. I think it was because I was beginning to feel in my bones that I wanted to work nearer home.

My next job was at Betterwear's order assembly warehouse, at Hartcliffe. Here I marked up loads for delivery by the firms vans, and helped to unload the supplies lorry, once a week, when some tons of goods were delivered.

Joan was now working in Burton's shop-cum-Post-Office in Symes Avenue, Hartcliffe. Denise was still at Hartcliffe school.

I went up to Somerdale Avenue every Saturday morning to visit mother and the rest of the family. My mother had the front room which was also her bedroom. I used to go into her room for a quiet chat about various topics. More often than not the subject would be times past, the Paice and Wall families. We chatted at length about her family line, her young days, and how leather stitching was introduced to her by her father. (See appendix. The Wall Family Line.)

When I was a young boy and listened to conversations between my father and mother, the "old un" was mentioned now and again. They were talking about my Grandfather Paice, and comparing his looks and resemblance to the "old un". Being a young boy and having other things on my mind, I did not pay too much attention to what was being discussed by my parents. But I did wonder who the "old un" could be. (See appendix. The Paice Line.)

My sister Joyce's two girls were in the St. John's Ambulance Corps, and the youngest, Josephine, was making progress.

# CHAPTER 21

1965 and the high rise flats in Symes Avenue were now completed and ready for occupation. We fancied living in the high rise so we applied for a transfer, which we got, and moved to the tenth floor of Middleford House. That was the top floor, with a lovely panoramic view. It was surprising, but the rooms were very spacious and well built, with central heating, and a laundry-room on the ground floor with drying facilities etc.

All together better than the one-up and one-down flats in Hareclive Road. We did not get any traffic noise or neighbour disturbance up on top. Joan had switched jobs, from Burton's to the Kiosk newsagents in Symes Avenue. I was still at Betterwears.

My backaches were now pretty bad and I had the occasional sick absence from work. My doctor sent me for an X-ray at Southmead Hospital. The X-rays showed that the cervical discs in my neck were deteriorating, and showing much signs of wear. I had degenerative cervical spondylitis. I was told nothing could be done about it; it was progressive and would get worse. I was told to change my job and seek a very light kind of work. I left Betterwear and started as a storeman-cum-progress chaser at the repair section of Bristol Siddeley, at the old Whitchurch Airport. Up to then, I had considered the job at Betterwear the worst I ever had. The new work at the hangars was split in two working sections, the Olympus jet engines, and the section for propellor engines. The jet engine section was on the south side of the former airport, the propellor section being on the north side. This north side was close to the bottom of Creswicke Road junction with the Airport Road. My brother Dion worked at the north side as an inspector. He worked on pistons etc, dye-testing for cracks. I started my work at the south side hangar, it was a heavy job, handling the components for the jet engines, and I knew that I was going to be worse off. This was much heavier than the Betterwear job. Luck was with me, however, as I was transferred to the propellor section on the north side within a month or so.

This job was not particularly heavy. I was on the line as a checker and progress-chaser, my work being mainly in the stores. My part of the action was to receive the parts of the engines dealing with the pipes, all types, metal, rubber, brackets, clips, feathering pipes, the propellor-cone retaining ring, various nuts and bolts. These parts were first examined by the inspector, to determine whether the part was still serviceable or required 100% replacement, and the engine's documentation sheet would be marked accordingly. All the pipe "bits" were sent to me, in a large red box, and when I received them I spread them out on my work bench. Then, with the documentation, I checked that every single piece, whether a pipe, even a nut was there. I had a range of bolts, nuts, screws, small components etc, to hand, in case there were any missing. Any pipes that needed replacing I obtained from the new-parts store. When I had the engine pipes ready, and cleaned up, if necessary, and all complete, I would take the box out to the fitters line, where those parts would be assembled, and then passed on up the line for the next stage of engine assembly. Depending on the amount of work required, I could do three sets of pipes each day.

My brother-in-law Joe had left Shattock's leather works and in fact worked on the same line that I was supplying. Other things I did in connection with this work, was to have some metal pipes and brackets, clips, cadmium plated and sometimes I needed to degrease new components. This was done by dipping the greasy component into a tank of special chemical liquid, and then washing it in water. I did not care for that part of the job, though, as the fumes from the tank were terrible to breathe in, and could prove fatal. Joe went home to Somerdale for his lunch each day, in his car, and Dion and I went with him and ate our sandwich lunch at mother's next door. Dion was living in Wellgarth Walk, just up the road from Somerdale Avenue.

On Saturdays I still visited mother.

After a long stay at North Side Hangar, I was sent back over to the South Side Hangar. So I was back to the heavy stuff again, which did not do my complaint any good. Although there were fork-lift trucks and trolleys, there was still a lot of manual handling to do. By the way, I think that in those days a complete Olympus engine weighed something like seven tons. Each day my work load was pretty consistent. One day, however, I was kicking my heels with nothing to do, so I went into the next store, to give a pal a hand because he was on his own and had a big job to do. It was a new parts store, separate from mine, but situated on the same ground, and it was all part of Bristol Siddeley. My section leader happened to pay the stores a visit and he saw that I was in next door helping out with their job. The section leader got his hair off at me and said "Don't let me ever see you helping out in there again." I was made to go back to my own pitch and twiddle my thumbs again. What nonsense, I thought to myself. The same firm, but no helping one another out. That was the way it was there though, all cliques and full of atmospheres.

One morning I awoke and had a sore throat but I went to work. It was a raw bitter day in March, and the cold really got to me. I was glad to see the day's work finished and get off home. I was by this time feeling quite ill. I went straight to bed with some aspirin. I had a terrible night with my throat hurting like mad, so my doctor was phoned to come and have a look at me. He came early evening and took a look down my throat. "My God, you've got a nasty throat there," he said. "It feels like it, my throat is closed over," I croaked back.

Tonsilitis was diagnosed, and the doctor prescribed antibiotic tablets. The chemist shop in Symes Avenue was still open, so Denise popped over to get the tablets. When the tablets were brought back I tried to swallow a tablet with a little water, but it would not go down because my throat was practically closed over. The doctor was called again and he prescribed an antibiotic in liquid form as prescribed for babies. I used to tilt my head back and let the mixture trickle its way down my throat. My throat and mouth had turned a bluish colour. After a week of the mixture, the swelling was diminishing and I could swallow tablets, but it was nearly a month before I was well enough to go to work. A neighbour in the flats who had come in to have a look at me, reckoned that I had Quincy, as she had seen it before. I could believe her too, it was nasty while it lasted, and it left an ulcerated cyst on my right tonsil. A classic aftermath of Quincy. The cyst persists to this day. I returned to work but did not wish to stay in that employment, so once more, I was on the move. I left Siddeleys on my 39th birthday, 3.5.68.

On one of my Saturday visits to mother I was given a photograph of my grandfather's mother, Henrietta Paice. It was a sepia-toned Victorian print of a smart, good looking lady. I was to borrow the print and make a copy, then return the original to mother. I made a copy and gave my brother Dion the original print to take back to mother. I had left Siddeleys, so Dion had more of an opportunity to return the print. Whether the print was lost by Dion or lost by mother I do not know, but when mother died in 1974, the print never came to light in her possessions. I visited Dion a while back on a Good Friday, and we spent hours looking for the print, just in case it had found its way in to his collection of photos. No luck, and Dion couldn't even remember the photo of great-Grandma Paice. I, or rather we, have gone to great lengths to locate the missing print, because I have mislaid my copy as well.

Donald's wife, Joyce, reckons that mother had a "clear out" of some of her things, a couple of months before she died. The missing print could have been thrown out in error. We will never know. I have a photograph of my Grandfather Richard Paice and Grandma Ellen Jane. The photo was taken whilst they were stood in their doorway in Hill Street during the Jubilee street party in 1936.

I had discussed the family history with my mother, off and on, for years, during my lunch-time and Saturday visits. I was on one of these Saturday visits when my mother said, "I have something for you seeing that you are very interested in the family history." Mother gave me a large brown envelope and said "It's all written down in there about your Granfer Paice and his secret." Mother signed and added the date to her statement. I read the statement and I then knew who the "old 'un" was who had been mentioned in the past. (see 'The Secret' chapter.) When I finished the Siddeley job, I couldn't get work which would suit my condition, no lifting etc. I was unemployed for twelve months and signed on at St. Andrews Church annexe for unemployed in Hartcliffe. Denise started work in Barclay Bank in Symes Avenue. Joan was still working for Kiosks.

One night there was a violent thunderstorm and torrential rain ran down off the Dundry Slopes, and into the stream, which became a raging torrent. There was a culvert under the main Bishport Road, through which the stream flowed. The stream emerged and flowed alongside Hawkfield Road. This night the culvert was blocked by debris coming down from the hills, which caused the flood water to overspill the Bishport Road, and surrounding area. Symes Avenue was soon under water to a depth of six or seven feet, the raging torrent flowed on down to Hareclive Road and along Hawkfield Road and along the Hartcliffe Way, past the fire station, and on toward Parson Street. All the shops in Symes Avenue were flooded and much stock ruined. Hareclive Road, had many flooded houses. A bus got stranded along Hartcliffe Way, so passengers got off, and attempted to wade through the torrent of water. A woman who got into difficulties was in danger of being swept away by the water, so a man waded out to help her. Before he could reach her he was swept away and drowned. The woman survived. The next morning there was the clearing up to do. The shop staff were kept busy all day mopping up, sweeping mud and debris out of the shop. Joan came home with blisters on her hands. After a few days everything was back to normal. The flood not only hit Hartcliffe, but carried right on down into Bedminster, and caused much damage. The East Street shopping area was also under water. In Keynsham, a bridge near the park was swept away by flood water.

As I was unemployed and had nothing to do besides perhaps shopping and housework, I enrolled for an oil painting course by post. The name of the school was The Famous Artists', based in Amsterdam. Assignments were sent out by post to the students and when they were completed returned to Amsterdam. The school provided all course literature and instruction for oil painting. Students provided materials, the subject was landscapes, and my tutor in Amsterdam marked my assignments 'good' but pointed out areas to improve on. When I finished the course I received a certificate.

I had now been unemployed for twelve months so the employment officer at the annexe sent me on a six-week course at Fishponds Rehabilitation Centre at Gill Avenue, to be assessed for a job in office work. I joined the class at Gill Avenue, in the education section. When the six weeks were up I was assessed as capable of handling an office job, in a sedentary situation. This is it, I thought. Now to get a job. I was offered nothing by the Employment Office, so I made my own efforts to find a job. Over the weeks and after writing about 40 letters to prospective employers, I received only four replies to attend for interview. I was now 40 years old and registered disabled. I attended each interview but was turned down. I believe the reason for this was my age and state of health. A job presented itself at the new Gateway Foodmarket store in Whitchurch Lane, putting up orders for the various shops. So I was back to manual work again. I wondered how long I could keep this up. But I need not have worried on that score, for at the end of my first week in my new job – on the Friday lunch time while I was home – the disablement officer from the St. Andrews Annexe, came up to our flat in Middleford House and asked if I would like to go on a course at Bath Technical College. The course was for seven months on office management and book-keeping. It was commencing on the coming Monday. One person had dropped out at the last minute and it was thought that I could fill that vacancy. All the chaps on the course were disabled in some way or another, but not restricted by travel and could get around under their own steam. In fact, unless it was known otherwise, they could be taken for able-bodied men. All the men were aged between 21 years and 50 years. The course was funded by the Employment Exchange. Needless to say, I took the opportunity. I went back to work that afternoon and told them that I would be finishing that night. If they wished to, they could phone the Employment Exchange about it.

The travelling details were given me on the Friday lunch time. A bus outside the flat would take me to St. Mary Redcliffe church, where I would board the Bath bus which stopped outside the college. An allowance would be paid weekly for myself and wife, plus the bus fares to and from the college. A claim needed to be put in weekly for the bus fares. When the college were on holidays, we had those days off. When we were away from the college on holiday, our allowance cheques were posted to us from the Employment Office. There were no deductions because of holidays. Usually we collected our allowance cheques each

Friday from the Bath Employment Office, just down the road from the college.

When my first morning came I caught the 7.45 bus to Redcliffe, then the 8.10 bus to Bath. The bus reached the college at about 8.55. We were shown our main class room which was in the old building. We gathered round introducing ourselves to one another. I had two chaps more or less travelling my way from Bristol. One chap's name was Busvine, he lived in Brislington and the other chap's name was Clifton, and he lived at Clifton. There were 12 of us on the course, and 10 finished it. Two dropped out half-way through. The first room we were shown on our first day remained our tutor room throughout, but we did use some other rooms occasionally.

The college had their own cinema which we visited a couple of times. As students we used the refectory for meals. I thoroughly enjoyed the course and was all too keen to sit the college internal examinations, and also examinations for The Royal Society of Arts. We were taught to type and I could manage this, but did not have a great interest in it. I never took the examination in typing, but did so for all the other subjects. I passed in bookkeeping, commerce, maths, English, in the college's own exams. I had passes and certificates, from the R.S.A. in commerce, English Language with Literature, and a pass in maths with credit. We finished the course at Whitsun, 1970. Before I forget, at the College we also did training on giving a speech or talk to an audience. We each prepared a talk on our chosen subject. In turn we stood in front of our fellow students to deliver the talk. I chose a talk on saddle-making and took some of my mother's stitching tools to the College. Another student gave a talk on car engines. A great time was had by all.

At Whitsun, Denise went on her first flight in an aeroplane. It was with her friend Jenny and her parents to Spain on holiday.

# CHAPTER 22

September, 1970 . . . I had started work with a building firm in their office. It was a boring sort of job, and I left after a couple of months. I thought that I would easily get another job with my qualifications. Not so, when I applied there were the usual 'put offs'. Too old. No experience. Poor health. I went down to the Employment Exchange Disabled Department, to see if anything could be found for me. There was not, and in the end, I was given a job in the very office that had put me on the course at Bath Tech.

I was now a Civil Servant. As a clerical assistant, my duties were to

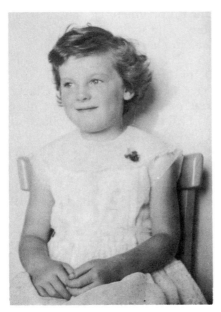

Daughter Denise, aged 9.  Denise at home: Hartcliffe flats, 1967.

Denise marries Alan Richard Hill at St Pious R.C. Church, Hartcliffe,
March 22nd 1975.

commence in the retraining section of the Employment Dept, which had an office on the fifth floor of The Pithay. The senior executive officer (S.E.O.) was a Mr. Maddocks who was in charge of the section.

In the office where I worked was the Executive officer Alan Cole. Other officers were Frank Coxall, Derek Hughes, Gordon Edwards, Betty Peche, Janet Britton, Frances Tyler, George Fowles, Ron Clarke, Jim Dolling, and a few more whose names I cannot remember. Basically, my job was documentation of all the incoming applications for retraining at the Skill Centre, in Fishponds and for college courses. Applications for retraining at other skill centres and colleges, in other counties were documented then passed on to the appropriate Employment Office for the area. I arranged panel interviews for prospective trainees at the Fishponds Skill Centre medical examinations by the skill centre doctor, and sent out the necessary forms and travel warrants as required. Some trainees as far away as Cornwall travelled up for the Panel selection interview at Fishponds Skill Centre, these chaps would have been trained, if passed by the Panel, at the Fishponds Skill Centre, and would have been placed in nearby lodgings. The Skill Centre maintained a list of lodgings available from local residents. I had other duties which were keeping up the stock of forms and other papers and re-ordering if necessary. All the things which could be found in a office I kept a check on. I was responsible for recording the sickness and holiday absences of the office staff, and sending the forms to Head Office at Runcorn. This was the job which suited me most and I had nice friendly persons around me. I was enjoying myself in my new job. I got on particularly well with Alan Cole, and could go to him with any problem and he always willingly sorted it out for me. He was, without doubt, the best chap that I had ever worked with. Alan's wife, Betty, also worked in the same department, but in a different section. Betty was a very friendly and likeable person, too. Alan Cole was into photography and the day that our 14,000th, application was received and documented he took my photograph, showing off the file. Now and again temporary staff were taken on and one such person was John Constable. In the evenings he worked at the Hippodrome Theatre on the Centre, as a dresser for the performers. He sat at the same office table as I. One day he asked if I would be interested in some complimentary tickets to see a show.

The show sounded as if it was going to be a good one. I accepted the offer of some free tickets. Who wouldn't? John gave me four tickets for an evening performance to see top stars of the day. There was Ivor Emmanuel, the great Welsh singer, Ron Moody, the Welsh comedian, and the popular group Herman and the Hermits with Peter Noon, and another comedian. It was a great show. At the interval, John appeared from behind the stage wings, came down to where we were seated and asked if we would like to go backstage and meet the cast. We were all for it, and trooped behind John to meet the stars backstage. We met and had a little chat with Ivor Emmanuel, Ron Moody, Peter Noon and the group, and we had a glass of sherry with Ivor, in his dressing room. We returned to our seats for the rest of the show. These were in the very first row. Of course the opportunity arose for a bit of comic banter, which was directed at us in the front row in the glare of a searching light. A good show all round, with splendid performances by all and the show ended with a magnificent tableau with Ivor singing a great song called "The Impossible Dream".

John Constable did not stay long at the Pithay. I think he returned to London. I have a feeling that his mother was on the stage, in London, as there was mention of Drury Lane Theatre during our conversations.

The big tremble. Joan, Denise and I were sitting in our living room flat on top of Middleford House, one Saturday afternoon, when all of a sudden the whole building shook and trembled for about 10 seconds. It was a frightening experience while it lasted, to feel the settee we were sitting on shaking, as the high rise flats trembled. The tremor was centred in mid-Wales, the result of a small earthquake. Joan and Denise started to cry, it was that frightening, but it did not last long enough to cause any long-lasting panic.

Denise had changed her job and was now working for a firm of solicitors, in town. Yes! You've guessed it. Joan was still working in Symes Avenue, but in a different shop. I had stayed in the job at Pithay for three years and was now yearning to see some different surroundings. I was not fed up with the type of job I was doing – just wanted some thing a little different in a new setting. My new work place was to be the Inland Revenue office, Washington House, on the lower slopes of Brandon Hill, in Great George Street. There was a lovely view of the parkland and also the city surround. Part of the river through Hotwells was visible and we were able to see the Great Britain being towed up river, when she was brought home from the Falklands.

At the Tax Office my job was in the section dealing with self-employed persons. The section also handled Trust Funds. One such fund was the Dawn James Memorial Trust Fund. John James of course, is well known to all Bristolians for his benefaction to the hospitals, and providing trips for the aged. This fund was seen to by a senior tax-man. Too complicated for an ordinary tax officer, who wouldn't have been allowed to touch it anyway. Whilst at the tax office I had to go on a short course at the tax office training dept, at Flowers Hill, Brislington. After the course I returned to Washington House.

It was on my second day back, that I received a message that my mother had died. Her age was 74 years. I was given two days leave by the tax office, and a day for the funeral as bereavement leave. Mother was laid to rest with Father and Keith in the grave at Greenbank Cemetery.

The few belongings of Mother's were sorted out and I received her stitching tools and some old photographs. The print of Henrietta Paice was not amongst them.

August 1974. Whilst I was away from the tax office, one lunch time there was a telephone message for me. Peter Dean S.E.O. wanted me to contact him, at the Pithay office. This I did by phone. There was a vacancy at the Pithay and they wanted me back in the office. If I was interested, then Peter Dean would make the necessary transfer arrangements. I had worked only about twelve months at the tax office and I didn't really know whether I was ready for a change or not.

It must have been because I was a bit down at the death of mother, that I didn't care one way or the other. I decided to transfer back to the Pithay. The set-up at the office had changed considerably and was known as The Manpower Service Commission. So although some things stayed as they were, a lot didn't, and a certain amount of training was required by me. Alan Cole was still there as were Derek, George, Frank, Betty, Janet, Frances, Ron Clarke, and others. When the department changed over to Manpower Service Commission, some of the staff had been transferred out to other departments. I soon got into the swing of things and I was back with old friends.

# CHAPTER 23

March 1975 . . . Denise married Alan Hill at the Catholic Church in Hartcliffe. The reception was held at the Arnos Court Hotel at Brislington. There were more guests on the Hill side, than there were on the combined sides of Paices and Wheadons.

Alan's brother Daniel Hill is an actor, and he has appeared in various things on television including "Waiting for God" as Harvey Bains. It was Daniel who gave the reading at the church when Alan and Denise were married. Apparently Daniel had written a series for television to be called "Habits of a Lifetime". The sitcom takes place in a nunnery. I have seen a short "trial" version, on tape, but it does not appeal to me very much.

When Alan and Denise were married, they rented a garden flat up in Redland. We visited them now and again.

Denise had a car which she called "Lucy" and was able to come and visit us in our new home, a bungalow in a new council estate in Inns Court, near Knowle. When Denise married and left the flat in Hartcliffe to live in Redland, we were left with a spare room, so the council offered us a new bungalow in exchange for the flat, which we accepted.

Joan and I used to worry when Denise visited us at Inns Court in her car. It was always nearly night time when Denise started on her journey, back to Redland and it was a longish run too, car or not.

Denise used to go home, from Inns Court down to Winterstoke Road, then along the Portway, up Bridge Valley road, on to Clifton then into Redland. Denise never minded travelling on her own, but her mother and I never got used to it. The thing was Denise hadn't a phone at Redland, so couldn't let us know that she had arrived home safely. To add to our worries Denise was expecting a baby, and we didn't like her making that journey to Redland at all.

Her son was born at the Maternity Hospital in St. Michael's Hill on March 4th, 1976. There was a fire alert at the hospital the night he was born, with fire engines racing all over the place. It was a false alarm, to everyone's relief. The baby was baptised Matthew Daniel Somerset Hill, by the Bishop at the Catholic Cathedral, Clifton. It was in the year that Joan and I went down to Mawgan in Cornwall to visit a lady who had taken in the young Wheadon family as evacuees during the war. Ivy was the lady's name and she took Joan, Betty, Royston and David under her wing, along with all her six children – Inez, Sylvia, Betty, Reggie, Owen, and Jim Goldsworthy.

Aunty Ivy, as Joan knew her, was very pleased to see us, and asked after the rest of the Wheadon family. There was much talk of the old times down at Gweek during the war. Aunty Ivy's older sons are farmers, and her daughter Betty worked at the Seal sanctuary in Gweek, near Mawgan. I was still having troubles with my neck and back. Something different was happening however, for I was getting an aching just below my left ribs. An appointment was made for me to go to the Bristol Infirmary to have some tests done. The previous night I had to take some capsules and not take any food or drink on the day of the tests.

When I arrived at the B.R.I., I was examined briefly by a doctor then given some fluorescent tablets to swallow. Then I was sent off to the X-ray dept, where I was given a Barium meal to take. The X-ray operator took pictures of my body from my throat down to my navel. I was standing, lying down, in all sorts of positions, and given further quantities of a milky substance to swallow as the X-ray plates were taken. After the plates were taken I was told that I could wait a couple of hours, to learn the results, or come back on a later day. I waited.

I was called in to a room where the doctor said that I had a lovely stomach and to carry on eating whatever I fancied. I went away feeling much relieved at the verdict. That occurred way back in 1976. I still get a certain pressure under my left ribs with slight aching even to this day.

71

My doctor reckons that most of my troubles can be put down to my Spondylitis. Believe me, it's a nasty complaint. Besides the aching and paining, it causes stiffness, pins and needles, headaches, even affecting eye focussing at times. I don't know whether my Tinnitus is a result of my bone troubles or not, but it does nothing to cheer me up. I am very grateful, however, to be able to get around under my own steam. I can walk about as long as I do not overdo it. Should the Spondylitis eventually prevent me from walking out, then I would really consider myself in trouble.

June 1976 . . . We were on the move again. The office staff were moving to a new office at Minster House in Baldwin Street. We took over the fourth floor. The ground floor was the Jobcentre and the foyer of the building. Floors 2 and 3 were occupied by Kay's mail order dept. The fifth floor was used by the administrators of the Dawn Memorial Trust Fund. The offices were spacious and well carpetted.

We were now settling in our new bungalow at Inns Court. There was one problem with the site, though. At the back of the bungalow are Creswicke playing fields. There was practically no drainage in that ground, and during heavy rain the water used to run off the field, and overspill into the back gardens. The first two years there, we were flooded out, in our back garden, with the flood water threatening to get in to our bungalow. It was only because it stopped raining that we were saved from being swamped. We had to wait until 1983 before the field was seen to and drainage pipes laid.

Matthew was progressing very well, and was a sturdy little chap. He had a baby-walker with wheels and he used to tear around the room at the Redland flat. When I watched him my thoughts went back to my childhood and the times when I had my Mickey Mouse bike.

Denise and family were not too long living at Redland, for they eventually moved out to live in a house at the Novers. The house was only 15 minutes away from Inns Court, so we were all now living close together.

Joan's father, Edward George Wheadon, had died in 1973. Ivy, her mother lived on her own in a high-rise flats in Bishport Avenue.

Ivy came over to our bungalow each Sunday to have dinner with us. Ivy used to tell us of her young days when she was on the stage at the Prince's Theatre in Park Row. Ivy used to appear in pantomime also. One pantomime was *Babes In The Wood*. Ivy was a very good dancer and won dancing awards (see The Baker Family). In 1977 Ivy Wheadon passed away in her friend's room at the Bishport flats. She was cremated at the South Bristol Crematorium, as was her husband Edward George. Their names are entered in the Book Of Remembrance.

In this year Denise and family were living in a flat at Middleford

Grandsons Matthew (6) and Andrew (3), 1982.

Andrew, 8 in 1987.
Matthew, 14 in 1990.

73

House in Hartcliffe. That was the high-rise flats where we all lived before her marriage. A little while later, Denise was expecting her second child, and at this time was given a house in Elgar Close, Inns Court. That house was just a couple of minutes away, across the road, from where Joan and I lived in Wilbye Grove. We all could not have been closer.

# CHAPTER 24

Denise's second baby was born at the St. Michael's Hill maternity hospital on April 10th, 1979. A thunder storm was in progress when the ambulance took mother and baby home. Joan and I were allowed to go along with them in the ambulance. The new baby boy was baptised at The Church Of Christ The King in Filwood, by Father Richard McKay and given the names Andrew Anthony Hill. Matthew was soon to attend the church school in Filwood. On his first day he was presented to his teacher, Sister Theresa, whereupon Matthew kicked out at her because he was afraid of being left there. Sister Theresa wasn't at all put out by Matthew's reluctance to stay. She took Matthew's hand and gently, but firmly, talked to him, about how he would like school as there would be many nice things to do and how he would get to meet new friends. Matthew was won over and gave no more trouble. Sister Theresa was a lovely lady and loved by all the children. The Sister was missed by all her fellow-teachers and all the pupils when she retired.

Andrew's first birthday, he was rushed to the Children's Hospital for a double hernia. He made a good recovery and was home in a couple of weeks. Matthew was settled in school and looked forward to each day there.

The months and years were rolling on, and I was beginning to feel the pressure of going to work, so I applied for early retirement on health grounds. This was granted and the customary medical was waived. After all, they knew all about my health troubles.

I retired on Friday 2.1.81. I received a lump sum and a weekly pension from the Civil Service and I claimed invalidity benefit. I was 51 years old.

Joan had an operation to remove varicose veins from her leg. Joan was in hospital only two days. It took a few weeks for her leg to fully recover though.

Andrew was having tonsil troubles and his tonsils were quite enlarged. He went into hospital, and had his tonsils removed. I think his adenoids were done as well. Andrew started school in 1983.

There was the same trouble as when Matthew started but Andrew got in to the swing of things pretty quickly.

Sister Theresa had by this time retired.

I collected the boys each morning from their house, and took them to school. Whilst I was up at Filwood, I did the shopping for Joan and Denise in the local shops. At 12 o'clock I went up to the school to fetch the boys home for dinner. At 1.30pm, I fetched them again to take them up for afternoon classes. At 4 o'clock I returned to the school to take them home. I was getting exercise and fresh air daily.

Denise started looking around for a job and later started as a temporary typist at various offices.

The boys started staying in to dinner at the school, so my trips to the school were cut down to two daily, to take them in the morning, and fetch them in the afternoon.

Denise was usually at home by the time we arrived back from the school each afternoon.

Andrew had a slight hearing problem so he always sat close to the teacher's desk.

Joan and I always attended the school nativity plays at Christmas time. The children put their hearts and souls in to the plays, and always gave a good performance.

The school put on a special show to celebrate the Jubilee of the school's opening. The staff and children gave a splendid show. Andrew was togged up to look like Father Richard sporting a beard and all. Modern songs in fine voice, were rendered by the children and there were "take off's" of television characters, which were very amusing and had the audience in much laughter. The hour and a half show was video-taped and also the service in the church, which followed later. Copies of the event on tape were available at £5 each and were a good buy and, needless to say, I bought a tape.

We also attended the school's sports day, which took place on the Creswicke playing fields. It was great fun and pleasing to see all the kids happy and enjoying themselves.

1983 . . . We awoke one morning to hear a clanking and chugging of motorised vehicles out in the field. We went out in to our back garden to have a look. There were three earthmovers. They had arrived to commence drainage operations in the field. First, they moved in line, scooping up the top layer of earth to a depth of a foot or so. They then piled up the earth in a corner of the field. This was repeated all over the entire field. The earth movers took their loads of earth back to the pile in the field corner, and gradually the pile grew to a huge earth bank. The bank of earth must have been some 25 feet high, by the time all the field's surface had been collected.

The intention was that when the drainage job had been done, the earth would be replaced. When the earth was scooped up from the centre of the field, a Roman farming settlement was exposed and work was suspended for the time being. The news spread like wildfire and soon the treasure hunters with their metal detectors were clamouring all over the field. By just walking across the field one could see bits of pottery etc. There was a well there, and an archaeologist from Bristol Museum was examining the finds. Other archaeologists were charting the size and layout of the farm and making sketches. Many coins were coming to light, some were counterfeit. I went over and had a chat with the person at the well. Whilst I was there the lady dug up a heel piece of a Roman sandal. Many stones were carried off by the locals to put in their gardens. The archaeologists were given three days to carry on with their dig.

When that time was up the drainage work was to continue. The team of archaeologists did what they could in the time left to them. The earth-movers resumed their criss-crossing and scooping in the field. After the field was scooped and levelled, other machines started to dig trenches of about three feet in depth, ready for the twelve inch diameter drainage pipes to be laid. All of the earlier treasure-hunters had long since departed. I always had been interested in the past, and seeing that I was a keen coin collector, I bought a cheap metal detector to try my hand at treasure hunting. As soon as I had delivered the boys to school and got the shopping home, I was out in the field hoping to find some coins. I went over to where the Roman well had been located. The hole in the ground was circled by stones and still easy to find. The first thing I found was a molar-tooth. Of course the detector never bleeped for the molar, but for an old rusted nail.

Also, there was a bleep for the ring-pull of a can of drink . . . perhaps the archaeologist was thirsty? I found nothing of note at the well, so I wandered away to search another part of the field. The bleeper was sounding all the time but it was mainly for modern metal objects. An old watch was brought to light but disintegrated in my hands. A silver christening spoon was found. After a while I switched off the detector to light up a cigarette. I was idly looking around and down at the earth when I spotted a circular object a few feet away from me and I felt a spasm of excitement as I went forward and bent down to pick it up. It was partly caked in mud, but I knew that I had now found something interesting. When I returned home I cleaned off the caked mud from the coin and was highly delighted with my "find". The coin was a Roman "AS" of the Emperor Hadrian, bronze, with the bust of Hadrian on one side and the other side showing the Emperor mounted on his horse, talking to his soldiers. I looked up the coin in a catalogue and discovered the coin to be of a very rare type. To think of it, that I actually found that coin, without the use of the metal detector!

But to find objects just lying on top of the ground was nothing unusual, there were plenty, and just "begging" to be picked up. Other "finds" were coins through the centuries, Roman, a Viking, Henry I, Elizabeth I, etc. Two Roman rings and brooch were found plus a small figurine of the Roman God "Pan" playing the pipes, which was cut from the metal lead. Altogether, I had accumulated some 650 coins (no gold), and I also finished up with a sword blade, numerous modern things such as silver St. Christophers and chains, coins, a French military medal, lead musket balls, and a bronze medallion of George V and Queen Mary to celebrate their Silver Jubilee. Many horse-shoes of various sizes were also found.

There had been a farm on this land for countless years and a couple of hundred years ago it was known as Phillwood Farm. Filwood Farm was finished in about 1938, when the Bristol Council bought the land for housing projects. During the war (1941) part of the once farmland was used to build 'pre-fabs'. The actual farmhouse site has yet to be built on . . . the spot is in the field corner about twenty yards or so away from where our bungalow stands. The field perimeter wire fence is our back garden fence. I wouldn't think that the field had ever been ploughed – anyway, not for centuries. I believe the field was mainly for grazing purposes. The field has been used for playing football even way back in 1938, when we moved up to the area from St. Pauls, and is now still a play area for football, cricket, golf and schools sports days . . . Once the field had been seen to we had no more flooding problems. The area was re-grassed and looked the same as it always had.

After the field was re-grassed, obviously, my treasure hunting came to and end. Matthew and Andrew occasionally came with me on treasure hunts in the surrounding fields but we never found anything interesting. I still had my job of taking the boys to school, plus the shop to visit. Matthew was eight years old and Andrew five years. For the next two years or so, I delved into the family histories of Paice, Little, Wall, Orchard, Merrick, Hughes, Rennolds, Bidder, Smith, Wheadon, Baker, Broomfield and Phillips. At the time of writing I have discovered my great-great grandmother's name was Chambers . . . another name to add to my ever growing list . . . connection being to the Smith family Isle of Wight. I paid visits to the Bristol Central Library and Record Office to search the records held there such as Births, Marriages, Deaths and Census. All of this information is on film or microfiche. After a spell of viewing the information on the 'viewers' my head used to spin and I felt as though I was going cross-eyed. Because of this I gave up using 'viewers' and concentrated on the written word for my information.

Joan and I have been to the Isle of Wight many times on holiday. We always found spare time to visit the Record Office in Newport, the island's capital (see Paice Family notes). We stayed at a small hotel in Shanklin and made this our base for holidaying and family research.

1986 . . . October. One evening we received a telephone message that my brother Vernon was seriously ill in Frenchay Hospital. He had a tumour on the brain which was inoperable. The doctors gave him a few weeks to live. We visited Vernon practically every day and towards the end he sank into a coma and died. Brother Vernon was laid to rest at Arnos Vale cemetery in the grave of June's father. I was glad that Vernon's suffering was finished. When I visited him at Frenchay I always thought back on our Dad and how he too had suffered before he died. Vernon died 18.11.86.

Matthew was now attending St. Bernadette's school, Whitchurch – Andrew still had three more years to attend Christ the King school at Filwood before he could move on to St. Bernadette's. Matthew went to school on a school bus daily from the church in Filwood. The bus brought home the school kids to the church each afternoon. The walk to and from the church took about fifteen minutes each day. We owned a video machine and taped some programmes from the television and also any good films. We also borrowed tapes from the local video library. It was at the video library that I learned that the old type 8mm. cine films could be transferred on to video tape. So I had my cine films transferred with appropriate music added in. My choice of title was Memories. Now, when we want to see our old cine films we simply put the video tape in to the video machine. The video firm made a good job of the transferring and it is nice to view my old films to the accompanying music . . .

Horse racing . . . I would not call myself a gambler, in the true sense of the word. I liked to have a modest bet now and then. My stake was low and I never, never stayed in the bookies, not even to listen or watch the race. I usually used to stake 20p a day and have an extra 10p on Saturday. In those days Saturdays, six or seven races were televised and they were called the ITV 6 or ITV 7. Bookmakers provided betting slips that covered the races. The bet was called the ITV 6 or 7 according to how many races were being televised on that particular Saturday. The bet could be to win only, or each way. The odds would be settled on the first selection, if a win or place, and then placed on the next selection at its odds. The object was to be successful, with all your selections right through the bet. Full multiplied odds applied with a consolation for five or six correct, 10% and 25%. One Saturday I picked out my selection for a ITV 6 and took my bet up to the bookies in Filwood. I staked 5p each way on my six horse bet, did my usual 20p and then went home. Later that day the races were televised. Joan and I settled down to watch the races. On my ITV bet the first horse won and the winnings would be placed on the next selection. My second selection won. We were beginning to get interested. The third won and we sat up and were really interested. The fourth came in and my accumulated odds were really high. The fifth came in and by now we were very, very excited. I worked out my winnings and had £2,724, going on to my sixth leg. The horse was 14-1 in the odds and I stood to win £45,860 if my last selection was successful. I shall never forget the name of that horse, it was Aniece, and I shall never forget my disappointment either, for my selection finished about 10th. But I picked up £270 as a consolation for the first five winners. This was worked out at 10% of my winnings, up to the sixth leg. Not bad for a 10p stake.

Football Pools . . . When I first started work at 14 years I did a few lines on my father's pools coupon for a couple of pence. I have been doing the Pools since 1943, except when I was in the Army. In 51 years, I have won three times; the total amount won would not amount to £5 . . . When I was in the Civil Service I won a £5 premium bond as a prize in a crossword puzzle. The bond never paid out a prize. In a competition by the Bristol *Evening Post* I won a copy of a book on Bristol's Docks. The authors were Frank Shipsides and our Bristol City Councillor, Sir Robert Wall. The book was signed by both authors. The title of the book is *Quayside Bristol*, published by Redcliffe Press of Bristol.

Family History . . . this pastime initially had me joining the local F.H.S. but as I made progress I found that all my ancestors, except one family, were out of Bristol, and in other counties. At the time of writing I am a member of the Hampshire Genealogical Society, the Isle of Wight Family History Society and the Hampshire Archives Trust . . . I have lapsed my membership in the local Bristol and Avon Family History Society.

One morning on waking, Joan could not open her right eye and had to more or less get her eyelids apart with her fingers. This was happening too often so Joan went to the doctor. He got the sister in the treatment room to take some swabs of Joan's eyes. These were sent off for tests and the results were negative. Opticians were consulted with the same negative outcome. Joan put up with this response with no improvement to her eyes, and they were still playing her up. Finally, I said "Right. Up the eye hospital we go and get this trouble sorted". So we went up to the hospital, where doctors examined Joan's eyes and they seemed surprised that no one had spotted what the trouble was. They told Joan that her tear ducts were not working. Therefore it was extremely dry eyes, and there was also a disease called Kerititis of her eyes. The dry eyes meant that Joan couldn't cry, even if she wanted to, for her eyes could not produce any tears. Treatment was Hypromellose (false tears) drops for her eyes six times a day. Another type of drops to combat the Kerititis was called Acetylcysteine and this was to be used twice a day.

Andrew was good at drawing and putting cartoon characters together to make a comic strip. He sat for hours on end drawing his cartoon strips. He would invent a character and make up a story, and then draw a series of pictures to make up a cartoon strip. Andrew bought the *Eagle* comic every week, and learned the fashion of comic strips. There was a competition now and again for youngsters to send their own cartoon strips. Andrew sent in one of his and it was published. Andrew received a prize of a "goody bag" with various things, such as "T" shirts, books, games and a golfer's cap. Matthew was into playing football and rugby at school and also becoming interested in golf. Denise worked a long spell as a 'temp' typist at British Telecom in Old Market. Matthew was 14 years old and Andrew was 11 years old. Matthew started walking to and from school, all the way, as he grew older. When Andrew transferred to St. Bernadette's he too used the bus from the church in Filwood to school but like Matthew he stopped using the bus when he was older. Matthew went on an "adventure course" in the Forest of Dean where all sorts of activities took place including canoeing, rock-climbing, cross country running, swimming etc. When Matthew came home he said "it was wicked" which to us old people 'past it', meant that he had a 'smashing' time and really enjoyed himself on the course.

## CHAPTER 26

April, 1991 . . . The ultimate thing for me to do regarding taking photographs and recording events and places, in motion and sound, would be to buy a video camera, which I did. The camera set consisted of the video camera itself, battery, a battery charger, a miniature size video tape and a 'caddy'. The 'caddy' was an adapter, the same size as a normal video, but with no insides, really an empty case, in which miniature size tapes of thirty minutes could be inserted. The 'loaded' case is played on a normal video machine just as an ordinary video-tape would be.

At first, only thirty minute tapes were available, but now forty-five minute tapes are readily available in the shops. The battery when fully charged would last one hour when videoing a scene etc. When the battery needed re-charging it was simply connected to the electricity mains; it usually takes forty minutes or so to re-charge the battery.

Our first opportunity to use the video-camera came when we went to

Leon and Joan in Old Village, Shanklin I-O-W, 1993.

Joan after the Camelot Show at Shanklin, 1992.

Thomas George Paice: headstone in West Street Cemetery, Ryde: died March 18th, 1865 aged 38 years.

Entrance, West Street Cemetery.

Looking down Union Street, Ryde towards pier. No. 7 bay window on right: Thomas George Paice, tobacconist/newsagent c.1852–65.

the Isle of Wight on holiday. The lovely gardens and the pier with the boat lake and esplanade were videoed plus the coming and goings of the hovercraft from Southsea and Portsmouth to Ryde. Ryde is where my Great Grandfather, Thomas Paice was in business, way back in Victorian times. His shop was in Union Street which is directly opposite the pier. The shop was about a third of the way up what is a long shopping street and a gradual slope upwards away from the Esplanade. It is the main shopping area for Ryde. We found Warwick Street where Henrietta lived when she was five years old with her mother Antoinette. Thomas' grave was located in the West Street Cemetery. The headstone was still clearly readable. At the top of Union Street, around the right hand corner, is St. Thomas Church. At the time, there was an exhibition to celebrate the First Fleet to Australia. In the church there was a display and a 'hologram' of a priest giving a sermon to his 'flock'. All this we were able to video, plus the font where Richard Paice and his brother William had been baptised. Their sister Hetty was not baptised at St. Thomas. I have yet to discover where. Hetty was born in Ryde though. We were very pleased with our first attempt at videoing, everything turned out splendid and we now had a record on tape of St. Thomas Church, Union Street, Warwick Street and the resting place of my Great grandfather, Thomas George Paice . . .

In the quest for family history, our travels have taken us to Hampshire and to Winchester Cathedral, Romsey, Michelmersh, Timsbury. Obviously, we took the video camera and recorded all the places we visited. Our videoing was not confined to other counties as there are many places near Bristol well worth visiting and videoing. Bath Abbey and the Roman Baths, Wells Cathedral and Bishop's Palace, to name a few, not forgetting our own magnificent Bristol Cathedral, St. Mary Redcliffe and Brunel's Suspension Bridge. We had a bonus when we were videoing Bath Abbey, for as we prepared to commence videoing, the choir assembled for practice.

Winchester Cathedral is a really magnificent building, the interior, a splendid awesome sight. Whenever I am in a holy place such as a cathedral or church, my days of being a choirboy always fill my mind. I have now got a second video playing machine, with this I can copy my miniature tapes on to a full size 4-hour tape. Therefore, 8 miniature tapes of 30 mins can be transferred on to a 4-hour tape. If it were 45 minute tapes that one was transferring, then the 4-hour tape would only take five and a bit miniatures.

April 1994 . . . Denise is working at London Life, in Redcliffe Way. Matthew has left school and is now in his second year of an engineering course at Bristol South College.

Andrew is approaching his 15th birthday. He wants to go to college, and do a course in art and graphic design.

He has recently been awarded certificates for best results for maths, in the school. The competition was in conjunction with Sharpes computers firm. Andrew received glowing reports for art and graphics.

Sept 95 Andrew has now commenced studying at St. Brendan's 6th, form College Brislington. His subjects are Physics, Maths, Design Technology, and Aeronautical Design . . . CAD.

Matthew has now finished his college course and done well in his exams. He also studies Socialogy at evening sessions. His aim is to read in History and Politics at University. He works at present, full-time in an office.

Alan, husband of Denise, is an excellent painter in oils and water colours.

Joan is 64 years of age, has a little blood pressure trouble but in no dire trouble with that.

I still ache with the Spondylitis and at the moment my shoulder wants to freeze-up. May 3rd. my 66th. birthday. . . . I still intend, if possible, to get about and visit places. Should I give a shrug of my shoulders now and again, its not braces slipping as I do not wear them. Its probably a move to pull my bones up together . . .

# THE SECRET

My Grandfather Richard Paice was born 14.8.1862 at No.7 Union Street, Ryde, Isle of Wight. His birth certificate shows that he was the son of Thomas George Paice, and wife Henrietta.

Records of the church registers for St. Thomas in Ryde, show that Richard and his older brother Thomas William were baptised at that church.

The boys had a sister, Henrietta (Hetty) but there is no record of her being baptised at St. Thomas.

Thomas George Paice was a tobacconist, newsagent at No.7 Union Street, Ryde, from pre-1853 until his death in 1865. He was involved in other business ventures in Ryde.

It was not known when exactly his widow came with her young family to Bristol, but it is on record that Henrietta re-married a William Eite, at the record office in Bristol in 1876.

Henrietta was then 40 years old and Richard was 14 years old.

The family lived in St. Georges Road, behind College Green.

When Richard was 15 years old he ran away to sea (step father problems?) and he returned to Bristol in 1882.

He married in that year, Ellen Jane Little, the daughter of a merchant seaman. Perhaps Richard, and father-in-law to be, had met while at sea? Richard and Ellen had 8 children. In early marriage they lived in the Easton district of Bristol.

In the early 1920s, the remaining family (some had married and gone their own way) moved to live in a house No.49 Hill Street.

My father, Charles Richard Paice was born in Easton on 18.2.1893. He married Doris Marjorie Wall at St. Clement Church in 1920. My father and mother lived at No.8 Hill Street opposite No.49.

In late months of 1936 my Grandfather Richard was ill with a cancerous growth in his mouth. The cancer was inoperable. My mother nursed him to the end. In his last days he used to ramble in speech. One afternoon my mother was tending the dying man, when he looked up at her and said "Doris, you have been so good to me, I am grateful for what you have done." He went on to tell her "I have a secret to tell you." The old man seemed to know what he was saying, so mother sat and listened to what he had to tell her. "Doris," he said, "I was an illegitimate child, my father was not Thomas George Paice". He went on to say, "my mother had a romantic fling with a nobleman and she became pregnant. Thomas George Paice was paid a sum of money to keep quiet about the affair and bring me up, as his own son."

Two days after my grandfather had told my mother his "secret" he died aged 74. It was January 1937. He was buried at Greenbank Cemetery.

As a boy I had listened to hushed snatches of conversation, about the 'old 'un', between my father and mother. My parents were discussing the resemblance of the nobleman with Grandfather Richard. "Yes," my mother would agree with my father. "Your father certainly looked like the 'old 'un'. Other snatches were about my mother's father, William Wall, and how he also agreed that there was a remarkable resemblance between the 'old 'un' and Richard Paice.

William Wall was in a far better position than most to express his opinion on the secret. For Grandfather William Wall was a journeyman saddler, and had worked in the stables of the big mansion in Gloucestershire, many times repairing saddles and other riding tack. He had often had a conversation with the nobleman (the 'old 'un'). William Wall married a girl who lived at Didmarton, two miles from the mansion. They were married in Bristol at Temple Church, near Victoria Street. They lived in a house at Fishponds.

When I used to go up to mother, when she was living in Willinton on her own, or when she was with Donald in Somerdale Avenue, we talked over past times and Richard's "secret". Mother reckoned that Thomas George Paice had used the money to start up his business in Ryde.

This can be discounted because Thomas was already in business for 10 years before Richard was born in 1862. Little bits were probably added in to the story as years went on. Like for instance, Thomas was a groom at the mansion's stables and Henrietta was a maid in the house. When Henrietta was made pregnant by the nobleman, Thomas was paid money to take her away and marry her. They went to the Isle of Wight.

My own research has shown this to have been impossible for the following reasons.

Henrietta was born on the Island. Her parents' names were John and Antoinette Smith.

Thomas George Paice was already on the Island in business in 1862, and had been for the past ten years. There was no mention of Thomas or Henrietta on the census 1861 for the house in Gloucestershire. They are on the Ryde 1861 census with son Thomas William and daughter Henrietta (Hetty).

Henrietta (mother) had never left I.O.W. and as far as I know, the first time Henrietta was not on the island, was when she was en route for Bristol . . . and why was Henrietta making her way to Bristol? Henrietta had left the Island after the death of Thomas George in 1865. In 1876 she remarried. Did Henrietta bring all three of her children to Bristol or just the youngest, Richard? This I have yet to discover. The noble classes spent many summer weeks holidaying on the Island in Victorian days.

# THE PAICE FAMILY – ISLE OF WIGHT

Thomas George Paice married Henrietta Smith at the Baptist Chapel (Castlehold) 13.4.1853.

Thomas was 26 years old, and Henrietta was 17 years old.

Thomas bachelor of Ryde, Tobacconist master.

Father . . . Richard Paice, a Wine Merchant.

Henrietta, spinster, of Ryde . . . Father, John Smith a seaman of Ryde. The marriage was witnessed by William Dyer and Eliza White.

Thomas in business at No. 7 Union Street. At one period between 1853–1858, Thomas and William Dyer were partners in the shop there.

The partnership apparently came to an end in later years. (White's Directory for Hants and the I.O.W. 1859 . . . Paice and Dyer 7, Union St. Ryde. Tobacconists-Newsagents).

Another Directory for 1846 has William Dyer at No 46. Union Street News Vendor. This William Dyer was a witness at his step-daughter Henrietta's marriage in Newport 13.4.1853.

Thomas George Paice organised and managed a New Year's Ball, Ryde 1859. He also managed public dances, at which the Ryde Quadrille Band played the music (extracted from the *Ryde and I.O.W. Observer* weekly newspaper, 19.1.1859 . . . The Record Office, Newport, I.O.W.). See also footnote "Terpiscordian Motion".

The same newspaper carried business advertisements on a regular basis for Thomas George Paice. e.g. *Tobaccos* . . .

*The I.O.W. Ryde Observer, Agent for the London Times, Maps and Guides of the Island, Picture-Cards. Newspapers delivered to all parts of Ryde. Newspapers lent to read at half price.*

Thomas George Paice also attended evening and dinner parties as a waiter. He was also involved in a boarding house business.

Henrietta had three children . . . Thomas, William born 29.1.1856. baptised at St. Thomas, Ryde . . . Henrietta (Hetty) born 30.11.1857, baptism unknown . . . Richard, born 14.8.1862. baptised at St. Thomas, Ryde. All three children were born at 7 Union Street in Ryde.

Thomas George Paice died at No. 7 Union St. 18.3.1865. He is buried at the West Street Cemetery Ryde . . .

It is not known how long after Thomas died that his widow Henrietta and the family remained in Ryde.

Henrietta remarried in Bristol 14.3.1876. She was then 40 years old.

88

Her son Richard was to become my Grandfather.

Research on the Paice family Ryde pre-1853 has proven negative so far. Details of Thomas George's birth and baptism are so far unknown as is his father's – Richard Paice, the wine merchant.

Richard and Thomas could have been born on the Island, but there is no record of this at the Record Office in Newport.

It is more than likely that Richard and Thomas had their roots in mainland Hampshire, or in any other of the Southern counties of England . . . perhaps even London.

The Census Ryde, 1861:

*7, Union Street.* Head. Thomas George Paice. Tobacconist. Master. Age 34 years, born Ryde . . . Henrietta Wife. Age 25 years, born Ryde . . . Thomas William son. scholar. age 6 years, born Ryde . . .

Hetty daughter. scholar. age 4 years, born Ryde.

The Thomas George Paice "born Ryde" bit is an error on the enumerator's part . . .

Based on my research, I wrote two articles for publishing in the I.O.W. Family History Journal.

One article is called "Terpsicordian Motion". The other is an account of my mother's leather stitching life, called "The Journeyman Saddler and his Daughter". See footnotes for these accounts.

I wrote a poem some years ago, based on the world we have to live in today, the appropriate title was "Tears of Shame".

On our visits to Ryde we easily found the street and premises once used by my great grandfather.

The St. Thomas Church is at the top of Union St. just round the corner, Warwick St. is a few minutes walk from St. Thomas Church. The West Street Cemetery, is a little bit further along the main shopping street from Union Street.

The grave of Thomas George Paice is near the Chapel, and the head stone of the grave is clear and readable. The Medina Council keeps the cemetery well tended, in cutting grass and clearing waste away.

An official of the Medina Council helped me locate the grave. He was very helpful, and even sent me photocopies of the burial ground registers which gave all details of the deceased, names, date of death and burial, the cost of the grave, the purchaser's name, plot number etc . . . He kindly sent photos of the grave.

At Newport the Lord Louis Library is in the town centre near the Bus Depot. Castlehold Baptist Chapel is in the next street (High Street). The Record Office is at Hillside near the Docks, about 10 minutes walk from the Library.

# THE BAKER FAMILY

Charles Henry Baker Senior was a monumental stone carver. He married Lucy Ellen Wall. The family lived in Hotwells.

The Baker family were all performers, on the stage of the Prince's Theatre in Park Row. Charles Henry Senior teamed up with a man to do a dual act. In later years, Charles' partner went solo, and appeared as the "Chocolate Coloured Coon" – this man, G.H. Elliot was to become a very popular singer. C.H. Baker's son, Charles Henry Junior, was a yodeller . . . Lucy sang soprano.

Gertrude played the piano and Ivy Victoria, my wife's mother, danced on the stage, and also appeared in the pantomime, "Babes in the Wood". In later years Charles Henry Baker senior became a cinema projectionist in Weston-Super-Mare.

C.H. Baker junior entertained the troops, when he was serving in the Army in the 1940s. Apparently, Ivy started when she was 14 years old.

Ivy became engaged to Edward George Wheadon in 1928, but was made to give up the stage, before he would marry her.

# THE WALL FAMILY (mine)

Arthur Edward Wall was born in Kingswinford near Walsall, the leather town in Staffordshire.

William A.E. Wall apprenticed in saddle making in Walsall. He became a journeyman saddler. Travelling down from Walsall, he worked as he travelled, through the Midlands and into Gloucestershire, then on to Bristol. It was while he worked at the big mansion, that he met his future wife, Rosa Ann Orchard.

Her father, John Orchard, was a coachman to the Duke of Beaufort. Rosa Ann lived at Didmarton Village, a couple of miles from Badminton House. It is possible that Rosa worked at the House as well.

I haven't yet discovered whether W.A.E. Wall and Rosa, as a married couple, lived at Didmarton or not. They finally settled in Sevier Street, Stapleton Rd. Eastville Bristol.

W.A.E. Wall then worked for Shattock and Hunter, saddle and leather works in Frogmore Street in the Centre of the City.

Joseph Wall, bachelor, carpenter of Brockmoor Staffs, married Susan Hughes, spinster of Brockmoor at Kingswinford, Staffs, 7.11.1859.

# THE WALL FAMILY (Joan's)

William Wall married Ellen Broomfield in Bridgwater, Somerset. William was a shoemaker. They left Somerset to live in Bristol.

Records show that they lived in Hotwell Road, and William had now become a quayside worker (a step down?).

Lucy Ellen Wall was born in Hotwell Road. There were more children and Ellen's mother from Bridgwater, Sarah, also lived with the family.

# THE SMITH FAMILY

John Smith, seaman and Antonetta Chambers were married on I.O.W. or Portsmouth or Southampton.

Daugher Henrietta was born, 1836. where unknown . . . Ryde possibly. Henrietta married Thomas George Paice at the Baptist Chapel (Castlehold) Newport, I.O.W. 13.4.1853.

Henrietta age 5 years, and her mother Antonetta, age 25 years living with Ann White age 30 years, and daughter Mary Ann age 10 years, in Warwick St. Ryde Census 1841. There were no males in residence (both at sea). Antonetta re-married William Dyer, tailor, of 46 Union St. Ryde. 13.10.1844. The shop was a newsagents in the Census of 1851. William Dyer, Head. Wife. Antonetta, a straw-bonnet maker. Henrietta, 'daughter' a shop assistant. Because Henrietta was listed as daughter to William, instead of step-daughter, this caused me a lot of time and wasted effort in my research into that family line.

# THE SMITH LINK (B)

Antonetta's parents . . . Her father was John Chambers a bricklayer of Ryde. Her mother was Ann whose maiden name was Smith. It is possible that Antonetta married a relation of her mother's, perhaps a cousin? This is Antonetta's first marriage, the husband being John Smith. William Dyer was her second husband . . . It could be assumed that John and Antonetta were divorced (if they were married that is). When Antonetta re-married in 1844 to Wm. Dyer, there was no indication on the marriage certificate that she was a widow. When Antonetta's daughter, Henrietta, was married in 1853, the certificate did not state that the brides' father was deceased.

## THE CHAMBERS FAMILY

John Chambers of Ryde, bricklayer, married Ann Smith at Newchurch I.O.W. Antoinette or Antoinetta or Antonetta Chambers was born 7.6.1814 at Ryde. Baptised 27.11.1832. (in a hurry to get married?) at Sun Hill Congregational Chapel, West Cowes, I.O.W. . . . First married . . . date/place unknown. Second marriage (as a widow? or divorcee) to William Dyer of Ryde, a tailor at the Parish Church Newchurch I.O.W. on 13.10.1844 . . . Witnessed by Alfred Chambers and Clara Chambers. Henrietta Smith was then Wm. Dyer's step-daughter.

## THE ORCHARD (ARCHARD) FAMILY

John Orchard married Anne Merrick (or Meyrick) at Oldbury-on-the Hill in Gloucestershire. John was born in Tetbury, Glos. Anne was born in Oldbury, the daughter of a John Merrick (Meyrick). When Anne was married, she was working as a servant in Tetbury. John moved to Didmarton and became a coachman at Badminton House. John and Anne had two children, Rosa Ann, and Emma Jane (died young). Anne Orchard died when Rosa Ann was quite young. John Orchard re-married Ruth Porter . . . there was no children from this marriage. John was working as a labourer for James Hatherall of Tetbury at age 21 yrs. John also signed-up for militia service when of same age.

## THE BIDDER FAMILY

Robert Bidder married Phoebe Rennolds in St. Mary Redcliff Church 11.6.1826. Daughter Jane married Edward Little, seaman. Son, Robert, a hatter.
Robert Snr. ironmonger of St. Thomas Street, Redcliff, Bristol.

# THE LITTLE FAMILY

Head of family . . . William Little, bakery tradesman of Stokes Croft, Bristol. Son . . . Edward, Seaman.

## NAMES LIST

Paice
- Richard I – Richard II – Richard III.
Thomas George – Thomas William – Henrietta (I) (Hetty) (2).
Charles Richard – Herbert – Donald Arthur Richard – Keith.
Vernon Garth – Leon Wilfred – Dion Gerald – Joyce Doreen.
Denise – Rose – Violet – Alice – Louise – Annie-Florence.
Keith II – Lee – Robert – Neil – Paula – Bernice.

Wall
- 'Paice Line' – William – Joseph – Arthur Edward William.
Stanley Hughes – Cyril – Wilfred – Arthur – Doris Marjorie.
Gladys – Stanley – Philip – Clifford – Johnny – Female Wall.
Evelyn – Jesse – Trevor – Maurice – Bernard.

Wall
- 'Wheadon Line' – William – Lucy Ellen – Sarah, Wife of William.

Broomfield – William – Ellen.

Wheadon
- Herbert John – Alfred E.W. – Herbert – Edward George.
Joan Kathleen – Betty – Royston – David – Michael – Martin.

D'Luz
- Emmanuel . . .
Phillips
- Alfred – Kate May . . .
Eite
- William Snr – William Jnr.

Smith
- (A) John – John Jnr – Henrietta.

93

| Smith | – (B) Ann . . . |
|---|---|
| Chambers | – John – Clara – Alfred – Antoinette or Antonetta. |
| Dyer | – William. |
| White | – Ann – Mary Ann – Eliza. |
| Orchard | – John – Rosa Ann – Emma Jane – William. Ruth? Second wife of John. |

Meyrick or Merrick – John – Ann.

| Hill | – Matthew Daniel Somerset – Andrew Anthony – Alan Richard. |
|---|---|
| Hughes | – Susan. |
| Little | – Ellen Jane – William – Charles Edward. |
| Bidder | – Jane – Robert – John. |
| Rennolds | – Phoebe – William. |
| Baker | – Charles Henry 1st – Charles Henry 2nd – George. Ivy Victoria – Gertrude – Lucy – Annie – Ellen (Nell) Thomas. |

# NOTES ON PERSONS MENTIONED IN THE TEXT

John Chambers – bricklayer of Ryde.

William Dyer – tailor in 1844 – but newsvendor at No. 46 Union Street in Ryde 1843 (Directory).

Charles Henry Baker – was a monumental stone cutter and polisher as a young man. Married Lucy Ellen Wall at Bristol Register Office.

Stage performers – all family, at The Princes Theatre, Park Row Bristol. Charles Henry Snr; became a cinematic projectionist at Weston-Super-Mare in later life.

Ivy Baker started on the stage, when she was 14 years of age – dancing pantomimes etc.

William Wall of Taunton, and Ellen Broomfield married, and in later years came to live in Hotwells, Bristol.

They brought their family and William's mother with them, William was a shoemaker in Taunton. He was a quayside worker when living in Hotwells.

Did John Smith and Antoinette divorce? John Smith was apparently alive, when Henrietta was married in 1853. No mention of him on marriage certificate. Could have been an omission?

Eite William – a labourer, his father Thomas was a farrier, at the Great Western Hotel, in St. Georges Road which later became a stables and Coach Dept.

Joseph Wall – a carpenter – Kingswinford – Brockworth Staffs.

Arthur E.W. Wall married at Temple Church, Bristol.

John Orchard – coachman to the Duke of Beaufort, his wife Ann, a servant. Ann buried at Didmarton. There is a plaque to her memory in the church at Didmarton. Didmarton – Tetbury – Oldbury-on-the-Hill, all within a few miles of each other.

Richard Paice – alive in 1853 – A wine merchant.

Not on 1841 – 1851 – 1861 Census for Ryde or anywhere else on the I.O.W.

Thomas George Paice – Not on 1841 or 1851 Ryde Census – But listed on the Ryde 1861 – as a tobacconist master – No.7 Union Street.

The Ryde Census for 1861 states: Thomas – Henrietta – Thomas. Wm. – "Hette" – all born in Ryde.

This is incorrect – Thomas Wm. – "Hette" and my Grandfather – were born in Ryde – No proof found yet that Thomas George or Henrietta were in fact born on the Island. All other facts have been established. White's Directory. Hants and I.O.W. – 1859 – also Victorian newspapers. Ryde Observer, 1853 – 1859 – and all church register records.

Thomas William and Richard my grandfather, were Baptised in St Thomas Church Ryde. – But where their sister "Hette" was baptised is still not known.

The birthplace of Richard – Thomas George and Henrietta (Smith) is unknown, also – why did Henrietta come to Bristol, after the death of Thomas George?

Richard, my grandfather, came to Bristol with his widowed mother. They lived in St. Georges Road.

Henrietta married her second husband, William Eite in 14.3.1876. It is not known where exactly.

Henrietta came to Bristol. Did her two older children, come to Bristol with her?

There could have been stepfather problems, because when Richard was 15 years old, he ran away to sea. He returned to Bristol, five years later at the age of twenty years. He married in 1882 in Bristol.

My Father – Charles Richard – was a carter, before he went into the Army 1914. – He joined the Glosters – saw service 1914–1918. Was at the Somme–Ypres, and was a supplies soldier, at some time as a carter with a pair of horses.

One day a shell exploded near the cart and horses. Dolly and Policeman were both killed. Father caught some shrapnel in his back.

Father thought the world of his horses, and I have seen tears in his eyes, when in later years he told how they had been killed.

Father was also in the trenches, and he was gassed. He had eye trouble for the rest of his life, and he had to visit the Eye Hospital often to have his eye ulcers treated.

When father came out of the Army in 1918 he went to ask for a job at a well known Bristol lemonade factory. It was said that an uncle of his was the owner or manager at the factory. That made no difference – Father was refused a job.

During my family research I learned that my grandfather had worked at a lemonade factory, as a stoker. Was the owner or manager a relative of my grandfather? Quite possibly he was.

It was during my family roots search, that I discovered more about the activities of Thomas George Paice on the Isle of Wight.

Thomas had the shop business in Union Street Ryde – it was a tobacconist newsagents, also selling maps, guides and cards.

Thomas organised and managed public dances and A New Year Ball in Ryde. He also acted as head waiter at evening dinner parties. No wonder he died young at 38 years of age. He must have worn himself out, with all his activities.

My Grandfather Richard must have gone back to sea, after he married in 1882 – for I remember my parents talking about how Richard came home from a voyage – and brought smallpox with him. He was put in an isolation Hospital, which was down on the river behind St. Phillips. All his furniture coverings and bedding and clothes were burnt in the street at Hill Street – Richard recovered.

# FAMILY TREES

RICHARD PAICE
THOMAS GEORGE
RICHARD
CHARLES RICHARD
LEON WILFRED
DENISE
..............................................

WILLIAM WALL
JOSEPH
ARTHUR EDWARD WILLIAM
DORIS MARJORIE
..............................................

WILLIAM ORCHARD
JOHN (1st Marriage)

JOHN MERRICK (MEYRICK)
ANN
..............................................

HERBERT JOHN WHEADON
ALFRED E.W.
EDWARD GEORGE
JOAN KATHLEEN
..............................................

THOMAS BAKER
CHARLES HENRY
IVY VICTORIA
..............................................

EMMANUEL d'LUZ
..............................................

WILLIAM BROOMFIELD

ROSA ANN (1st Born)
EMMA JANE (2nd Born)
  ... (JOHN ORCHARD) 2nd
  Marr. to RUTH PORTER? ...
(children?)
..............................................

WILLIAM LITTLE
CHARLES EDWARD
ELLEN JANE
..............................................

ROBERT BIDDER
JANE
..............................................

"A"  JOHN SMITH
    HENRIETTA
..............................................

"B"  ANN SMITH (marr.?)
    ANTOINETTE
..............................................

ELLEN
..............................................

WILLIAM WALL
LUCY ELLEN
..............................................

WILLIAM RENNOLDS
PHOEBE
..............................................

JOHN CHAMBERS
ANTOINETTE
..............................................

SUSAN HUGHES
..............................................

ALAN RICHARD HILL
MATTHEW DANIEL
  SOMERSET (1st)
ANDREW ANTHONY (2nd born)
..............................................

"A" = 1st. line as follows
"B" = 2nd. line as follows

ANTOINETTE SMITH – married first to John Smith and second to Wm Dyer.

| NAME | BORN | MARRIED | DIED |
|---|---|---|---|
| RICHARD PAICE | | | |
| THOMAS GEORGE | 1827 | 13 4 1853 | 18 3 1865 |
| RICHARD | 14 7 1862 | 31 5 1882 | 7 1 1937 |
| CHARLES RICHARD | 18 2 1893 | 25 9 1920 | 15 7 1953 |
| LEON WILFRED | 3 5 1929 | 28 7 1951 | |
| DENISE | 30 5 1952 | 22 3 1975 | |
| HERBERT JOHN WHEADON | | | |
| ALFRED E W | 1879 | 2 2 1903 | 25 9 1915 |
| EDWARD GEORGE | 15 3 1906 | 22 6 1929 | 7 6 1973 |
| JOAN KATHLEEN | 21 10 1930 | 28 7 1951 | |
| JOHN SMITH (A) | | | |
| HENRIETTA | 1836 | 13 4 1853 | |
| ROBERT BIDDER | 1800 | 11 6 1826 | |
| JANE | | | |
| WILLIAM LITTLE | | | |
| CHARLES EDWARD | | | |
| ELLEN JANE | 19 12 1863 | 31 5 1882 | |
| JOHN CHAMBERS | | | |
| ANTOINETTE | 7 6 1814 | | |
| WILLIAM WALL (P) | | | |
| JOSEPH | 27.6. 1835 | 7 11 1859 | 3 5 1877 |
| WILLIAM ARTHUR | | | |
| EDWARD | 9 8 1860 | 6 4 1885 | |

97

| NAME | BORN | MARRIED | DIED |
|------|------|---------|------|
| DORIS MARJORIE | 30  1 1900 | 25  9 1920 | 7  4 1974 |
| SUSAN HUGHES | 1833 | 7 11 1859 | |
| WILLIAM BROOMFIELD | | | |
| ELLEN | | | |
| WILLIAM ORCHARD | | | |
| JOHN | 29  5 1831 | 25  7 1854 | 23 10 1917 |
| ROSA ANN | 4  7 1861 | 6  4 1885 | |
| EMMA JANE | 3  7 1863 | | 22  2 1866 |
| JOHN MEYRICK (MERRICK) | | | |
| ANN | 25  2 1828 | 25  7 1854 | 13  4 1865 |
| WILLIAM RENNOLDS | | | |
| PHOEBE | 1794 | 11  6 1826 | |
| ALAN RICHARD HILL | 23  1 1950 | 22  3 1975 | |
| MATTHEW DANIEL SOMERSET | 4  3 1976 | | |
| ANDREW ANTHONY | 10  4 1979 | | |
| THOMAS BAKER | | | |
| CHARLES HENRY | 1881 | 28  1 1902 | |
| IVY VICTORIA | 6  4 1905 | 22  6 1929 | 29  3 1977 |
| ALFRED PHILLIPS | | | |
| KATE MAY | 1880 | 2  2 1903 | |
| WILLIAM WALL (W) | | | |
| LUCY ELLEN | 13  5 1883 | 28  1 1902 | |
| ANN SMITH (B) | | | |
| EMMANUEL d'LUZ | | | |

'P' = PAICE LINE
'W' = WHEADON LINE
SMITH 'A' LINE = JOHN LINE
SMITH 'B' LINE = ANN LINE

| | | | |
|------|------|---------|------|
| RUTH PORTER? second wife of John Orchard no known children | 11  5 1847 | 11  2 1867 | |

# Articles by Leon Paice published in the Isle of Wight Family History Journal

# The Name is almost the Same

For years I had been unable to establish my Gt. Gt. Grandmother's surname. My Gt. Grandmother's surname was SMITH and the 1841 Census for Ryde listed the following:– Warwick St. Ryde. ANN WHITE – 30 years. Dau MARY ANN – 10 years. ANTOINETTE SMITH – 25 years. Dau HENRIETTA – 5 years. All born Ryde. Henrietta was my Gt. Grandmother. There were no males listed. Henrietta's father was a seaman, so was probably away at sea at the time of the census, as was Ann WHITE's husband.

I foolishly assumed Antoinette to be related to Ann WHITE, perhaps her sister. Much time and effort was wasted on searching for an Antoinette WHITE's marriage to a JOHN SMITH – Henrietta's father. Some time was also spent in looking for a baptism for an Antoinette WHITE. Also I have yet to obtain details of Henrietta's birth and baptism. I checked the Master Index on Marriages and Baptisms at the Newport Record Office. Nothing was found on Antoinette, John SMITH or Henrietta. Was the information incorrect on the 1841 census? I have the seven volumes I.O.W. Census Index – 1851, but could find no John Smith, Antoinette or Henrietta.

It was whilst I was researching my Gt. Grandfather's activities on Wight – pre 1853/1865, by way of Victorian Ryde Observer newspapers and White Directory to Hants/I.O.W., that I discovered that Thomas George PAICE, Tobacconist-Newsagent, of 7 Union Street, Ryde, had a partner in the business. White Directory 1859 shows a William DYER as partner.

Time passed by and I was no nearer finding my Gt. Gt. Grandmother's surname. I have a copy certificate marriage of Thomas George PAICE and Henrietta SMITH. They were married on 13th April 1853 at the Baptist Chapel (Castlehold), Newport, Isle of Wight. Thomas aged 26 years, Henrietta aged 17 years. Thomas's father was Richard PAICE, a wine merchant. Henrietta's father was John SMITH, a seaman. All Ryde residents. Witnesses were an Eliza WHITE and William DYER.

I looked at the Ryde 1851 Census Index and noted all DYER families with a William as head of family. I had often wondered whether one of these William DYER's could have been the partner to Thomas George PAICE in the business at no 7. Union Street, Ryde. Also the same William DYER who acted as a witness at Thomas and Henrietta's marriage. In the index I noted a family of three persons – William – head, wife Anett and Henrietta daughter. I was struck by the similarity of names, Anett was near enough to Antoinette and her daughter's name of Henrietta was right on and the fact that a William DYER had been a PAICE partner plus being a marriage witness made things more interesting. There was only one thing that could have turned me off, and that was the ages given in the census for the two females. Those were Anett – 33 yrs and Henrietta – 13 yrs. In 1851 Henrietta would have to be 15 yrs and her mother Anett (or Antoinette) would have to be 35 yrs. This did not deter me, as errors do occur in transcribing from original records. The census stated "All born Ryde" which could be incorrect also. I had no luck on previous attempts to find Henrietta's birth/baptism in Hampshire or Wight.

I was determined to follow up my theory – Antoinette had a second marriage. Was this the case? John SMITH had died? Or were they divorced? I checked the marriage certificate for Henrietta 1853. John SMITH – father was then alive. So, it must have been a divorce. I then applied for a search of the HGS Marriages Index – a William DYER and Antoinette SMITH (or Annett) 1841/45. Sure enough a marriage was found. William DYER and Antonetta SMITH on 13th October 1844 at the Parish Church, Newchurch, Isle of Wight. I then applied for a copy marriage certificate which gave me the information I had long sought for: William DYER – full age – Bachelor – father Daniel DYER – fisherman of Ryde to Antonetta SMITH – full age – Spinster – father John CHAMBERS – bricklayer of Ryde. Witnesses – Alfred CHAMBERS and Clara CHAMBERS. William DYER – occupation – Tailor.

As a follow up I obtained a census copy from the original records for Union Street, Ryde – 1851, which shows No 46 Union Street, Ryde – William DYER – head – newsvendor – age 34 – born Ryde. Wife – Antoinetta – age 33 yrs – strawbonnet maker – born Ryde. Daughter – Henrietta – shop assistant – age 15 yrs – born Ryde. A directory for 1843 shows that there was a William Dyer – newsvendor at No. 46 Union Street, Ryde. So now I knew that my Gt. Gt. Grandmother's surname was CHAMBERS. Other information learned from this was Antonetta – daughter of John and Ann CHAMBERS (formerly SMITH) Yes! another SMITH. Antonetta born 7th June 1814 Ryde. Baptised in West Cowes Congregational Sun Hill Chapel on 27th November 1832 (age now 18 yrs). I have been advised that Antonetta was preparing for marriage and had to be baptised quickly. Final thought. Did Antonetta marry a cousin named John Smith? and where did the marriage take place? There is not one in the records or master index at Newport Records Office. They could have been married perhaps in Southampton or Portsmouth?

I have explored the possibilities also on my Gt. Grandfather Thomas George PAICE and Richard PAICE pre 1853 in Ryde without success. Any information on these two gents pre 1853 also the Ryde Quadrille Band pre 1865 would be gratefully received.

---

*Has any member any information on the following? I would be grateful for any* information, however little.

The Ryde Quadrille Band c.1895.

I am still looking for the burial place and date for THOMAS GEORGE PAICE who died 18th March 1865 at No 10, Union Street, Ryde.

'*A Puzzler*' Can anyone sort this out?

I am searching for the *baptism* place and date for 'HETTY' whose full certificate of birth details are here noted:–

30th November 1857 HENRIETTA (HETTY) PAICE, daughter of THOMAS GEORGE and HENRIETTA PAICE, born at No 7, Union Street, Ryde. Informant was mother, HENRIETTA, and the address of the informant was The Strand, Ryde. Occupation of father was a lodging house keeper.

HETTY's two brothers, WM. and RICHARD were baptised at St. Thomas Church, Ryde, but where was she baptised?

---

Mrs Lloyd's account of Wight photographers trading in Victorian days (Journal 29) made very interesting reading. Noted the fact that there were five photographers trading in Ryde alone, four being in Union Street and one in Pier Street (Cravens Directory 1857). My Great Grandfather Thomas George Paice had a tobacconist/newsagents business at No 7 Union Street 1853/1862. He also organised public dances with the Ryde Quadrille Band (Ryde Observer Jan 1859) An account of this was published in the Journal about two years ago titled Terpiscordian Motion.

I often visit Wight and have searched in vain for a photograph of the band, possibly also portraying Thomas George Paice. My search has also been for a photograph of the Union Street shop-front again with possibly Thomas Paice stood outside. I recently purchased a copy of "The Way We Were" Vol. 3. There was a picture printed in the book showing Union Street looking up. The first shop on the left shown (low frontage) I could believe is my Great Grandfather's. There is a man stood in the doorway who could have been my Great Grandfather. It is only guesswork really as the picture is not too clear.

In 1858–59 Thomas had a partner named William Dyer. The nameboard hanging outside the shop is not too clear. I would like to think it reads 'Paice & Dyer' (White's Directory 1859). I am pretty sure this picture is of No 7 Union Street as I have compared the building's layout with my own photographs.

William Dyer was a news vendor at No 46 Union Street (now Threshers) in 1843. Thomas Paice married Henrietta Smith at Castlehold Baptist Church, Newport in 1853.

Should any member have knowledge of the photographs required I would be grateful to hear from them.

Thank you.

# The Journeyman Saddlemaker – and his Daughter

My Mother was DORIS MARJORIE WALL, the daughter of ARTHUR ED. WM. WALL. While working at Didmarton, near Badminton House, the home of the DUKE OF BEAUFORT, he had met ROSA ANN ORCHARD. They eventually married at Temple Church, Bristol. ROSA ANN's father was JOHN ORCHARD of Tetbury, Gloucestershire, who was coachman to the DUKE OF BEAUFORT in the 1880's. JOHN's wife was ANN MERRICK.

## SADDLERS' TOOLS.

This is a short account of the working lives of my Mother and her Father. My Grandfather had great pride in his work and so did my Mother, if not more so. It was skilled, but hard, work, and the end results were most satisfying for them. Of course, in their trade, years ago, it was all hand stitching of leather requiring skill and patience. Modern trappings can hardly be so satisfying. We have imitation leather, plastics, metal rivets and mostly machine stitching. So it is with respect and great admiration for the skill of my Grandfather and my Mother, who put everything into their work, that I now begin the story.

The saddlemaker lived with his wife and very young family in Walsall, in late Victorian England. Although he had commenced his trade in that small town it was a necessity of the times for a journeyman saddler to travel around the country to where work was available. In the early 1920's the need for saddlemaking and leather bridle work was beginning to slump. The advancing mechanical situation was making its impact on everyday life. My Grandfather was forced to move from place to place to follow his trade, his family went with him, and they finally came to Bristol and settled here.

Grandfather continued his trade working for a Bristol Saddlery and leather firm, located in Frogmore Street, Bristol. When the GREAT HOUDINI appeared at the Bristol Hippodrome my Grandfather would undertake the stitching of special sets of leather harness for HOUDINI's escape acts.

When my Mother was a young school girl she often had to rise early to deliver repaired leather work to Grandfather's customers. Some of these customers lived considerable distances from my Grandfather's house and my Mother had to make the deliveries and then race back to reach school on time. My Mother was considered to be a bright scholar and therefore expected by her Headmaster to go on to great things. Her parents, who could not afford extra school fees, etc., had different ideas about her future schooling, they expected her to follow in the working life of the Leather Trade. Although my Mother's Headmaster implored her parents to allow her to further her education, even with the possibility of a scholarship, her parents would not relent. My Mother used to tell us of that dismal part of her young life and spoke of tears in the Headmaster's eyes as he failed to convince her parents of her outstanding prospects. She never really forgave her parents for denying her the chance of a better education.

My Mother left school to take up work in the leather stitching trade and as she grew older, gained experience of the trade, she became very adept and became a quality leather stitcher. Often she actually worked on parts of saddles and heavy black harness, which was really considered to be a man's job. When my Grandfather died my Mother continued working in the leather trade. She now had her own young family to bring up as well as doing work on saddle skirts, girths and bridle work. It was very hard work and I remember seeing her hands often cut by the threads as she worked on the leather. At one stage my Mother and Sister would work at home. I can still see the gas-lit room with them

313. Stitching Horse.

sat at a table stitching harness which was held in position by wooden clamps. This was when I was a small boy and even then I played my small part. Threads had to be made and to save the stitchers time I used to make them. I still remember my bits for making the threads. I wore a small leather apron and the procedure was for me to have a hook in the wall and then run three turns of hemp around the hook to a length of five feet. This made six strands and each strand was beeswaxed together and rolled against my leather apron to make one nice waxed thick thread.

The Second World War was now on and my Mother and Sister went back to work with the Bristol Leather Firm. Some of the work they turned out was Sam Browne Belts for British Officers. They also did various work for the Americans and even stitched high white snow boots for the use of the Russian Army.

In my Mother's later years she took to doing work at home again and she

103

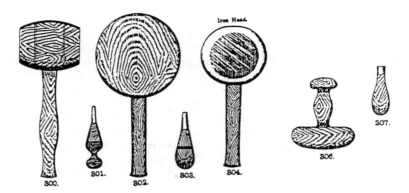

Iron Head

300. 301. 302. 303. 804. 306. 307.

received piece work rates, all the same it was very hard work. But it was a thrill to watch her hands flying in the stitching process. She worked with a thread with a needle and an awl in her right hand, the other needle in her left hand. A quick movement to pierce the leather with the awl and then to push the right needle through the hole then from the opposite side the left needle was pushed through the leather, both ends of the thread were then pulled taut and the process repeated. At times buckles and various rings or straps were added and stitched into position.

My Mother is dead now and with her went the family's interest in leather stitching. Although my Sister was very much involved some years ago she does not do any leather stitching now, her husband had worked as a leather cutter for my Grandfather's firm years ago. Myself, I was never really into the age of the family trade, apart from my small contribution of thread making. My working life up to now has been labouring, tyre-examiner, Progress Stores in the aircraft industry, finally finishing up working for the Civil Service. Needless to say all of my jobs were in Bristol and unlike my Grandfather I did not have to travel around the country to earn my living.

At home I have a wooden box containing some of the tools of the trade which belonged to my Grandfather. There are various marking and cutting blades, a pair of bulldog pliers, a slim tamping hammer, needles, leather pullers and a number of wooden-handled awls. Most of the wooden handles of these tools are well worn, cracked and there is some woodworm in them. When I look at the tools I visualise again the scene of the stitchers, with flying fingers, skillfully stitching and forming the leather into shape. Those fingers are now still. All that I have left are their tools and my memories of the Journeyman Saddlemaker and his Daughter.

48. Saddlers' Plyers. 47. Saddlers' Pincers.

104

# 'Terpsicordian Motion'

This account was extracted from the Ryde Observer, Saturday 17th January 1857 entry.

'A Public Ball, under the management of Mr. T. Paice took place on Monday, and it was respectfully and rather numerously attended. The hall was tastefully decorated with evergreens and floral devices etc., and it presented a very good appearance. The Ryde Quadrille Band attended, whose lively and excellent music kept the party in Terpsicordian Motion until a very early hour. The hilarity which prevailed proved the party was pleased, and certainly nothing was absent to contribute to their comforts, as the refreshments were bountiful and excellent.'

*Also Noted* Each edition carried an advertisement for 'T Paice Agent for London Newspaper Office at No 7 Union St., Ryde. Newsagents and Stationers. The Times supplied to purchasers at 2s/6d per week: Lent to read at 1s/-d. per week: Second day at half price and sent to all parts of the Town. Agent for the Isle of Wight Observer. Fashionable arrival list. Maps, Views and Guides of the Island. Mr Paice also attends as waiter at Dinner and Evening Parties'.

THOMAS and HENRIETTA had three children.

THOMAS WILLIAM 29th January 1856
HENRIETTA          30th November 1857
RICHARD            14th July 1862 (My Grandfather)

Each birth was announced in the Observer.

'At Ryde, Wife of Thomas Paice, a Son 29.1.1856'.
'At Ryde, Wife of Thomas Paice, a Daughter 30.11.1857.
'At No 10 Union St. Ryde, Wife of Thomas Paice, a Son 14.7.1862'.

Thomas died at No 10 Union St. Ryde – 1865. Aged 38 years.

---

Joan and I were on an August holiday in Wight and we had decided to spend a half-day visit to Newport Record Office. Roy Brinton, Hon. Curator of Carisbrooke Castle Museum advised that we visit the Record Office and look at the records held there.

With only a few hours we had allowed ourselves, we decided to look at the Victorian newspapers only. The staff produced the Ryde Observer (published weekly) c.1855–1863, therefore $9 \times 52 = 468$ copies of the newspaper. We read as much as possible in the time available.

We were delighted with what we did find, and it adds to the ventures of Thomas Paice of Ryde.

If it had been possible to read every copy of the Ryde Observer I am sure that more would have been learned of a somewhat enterprising man!